This book is to be returned on or before
the last date stamped below.

D0228091

Other Titles in the Better Business Series

How to Start and Run Your Own Business, 6th edition 1988, M. Mogano
How to Start and Run Your Own Shop, 2nd edition 1988, P. Levene

Better Business Series

How to Give a Successful Presentation

A Concise Guide for every Manager

Ian Richards

Graham & Trotman
A member of the Kluwer Academic Publishers Group
LONDON/DORDRECHT/BOSTON

Published in 1988 by

Graham & Trotman Limited
Sterling House
66 Wilton Road
London SW1V 1DE
UK

Graham & Trotman Inc.
Kluwer Academic Publishers Group
101 Philip Drive
Assinippi Park
Norwell, MA02061
USA

British Library Cataloguing in Publication Data

Richards, Ian
How to give a successful presentation.
1. Business firms—Management—Information.
Presentation—Manuals
I. Title
658.4'038

ISBN 1-85333-075-2
ISBN 1-85333-087-6 Pbk
ISBN 1-85333-088-4 Series

Library of Congress Cataloging-in-Publication Data

Richards, Ian
How to give a successful presentation: a concise guide for every manager/
by Ian Richards.
    p.   cm.
Includes index.
ISBN 1-85333-075-2 : £12.95   ISBN 1-85333-087-6 (pbk.) : £5.95
1. Business communication.   2. public speaking.   3. Business report writing
I. Title.
HF5718.R526 1988
658.4'5—dc19   88-824 CIP

Typeset in Great Britain by Cambridge Photosetting Services
Printed and bound in Great Britain by Billings, Worcester

Contents

Preface

Do I need a book like this?

If you ever have to stand up and talk to your colleagues, or more crucially, your senior management, the answer must be – Yes.

A few minutes in a high profile role can be worth more to your career than months of accumulated effort. A disastrous presentation can cause irreparable damage to your prospects and credibility.

Have you noticed that some people seem to be able to give lively and interesting presentations, while for others the whole thing falls flat?

You might have thought it was a gift, or put it down to a naturally extrovert personality. You would be wrong.

Have you noticed that some presentations have a professional polish to them, while others are clumsy and disjointed?

You might have put it down to some indefinable quality that comes with years of experience. Again, you would be wrong.

Does the thought of having to talk in front of your peers and senior management make you anxious?

You have nothing to worry about. *Anybody* can give an interesting, effective presentation.

To bring your presentation up to professional standard you just need to learn a few simple techniques. Once mastered, these techniques will enable you to stand with confidence in front of any gathering and make your case effectively, and impressively.

This book takes you step by step through all the stages of preparing and giving a presentation. Techniques that work are explained clearly and simply along with the reasons why they work. Jargon is avoided, but well known phrases describing established concepts are introduced and explained, enabling you to relate to other, more formal books on the subject.

All the stages of preparation are described clearly and simply. You will be taught how to plan a talk, how to make effective and impressive visual aids and how to pick the right type of aid for the job in hand.

As for the talk itself, you will be shown how to present yourself in the right way, how to interest and involve the audience and how to handle the inevitable awkward question.

In short, you will be given scores of hints and tips on how to give *your* presentation that professional polish.

How do I use this book?

To start with read it through. You will gain a thorough grounding in presentation techniques.

At the end of each section is a summary. When you are in the course of preparing a presentation, you can use these summaries to refresh your memory on the important considerations at each stage.

You will also be able to use this book as a reference guide. If you should be unsure of which approach is correct in a given circumstance, turn to this book. It is structured so as to give you ready access to the information required.

Introduction

The ability to give a presentation is a skill. In this respect it is similar to carpentry, driving a car, doing a crossword, cooking, or writing a letter.

Giving presentations, just like driving a car, requires the sort of skill that anyone of sound health can acquire to a reasonable degree of competence. With this book, some effort, and a little practice you will be able to stand with confidence in front of any gathering. Of course, just as some learner drivers go on to become steady, reliable drivers and others go on to race at Le Mans the standard which you achieve will depend to some degree on your natural abilities. You may be thinking of the drivers that go on to become a danger to other traffic. But they are the ones that forget the rules.

There will be those that give presentations without taking such advice as is to be found in this book. They will continue to splutter and stall at the side of the road while you glide past with your new found skill.

Before you are allowed to sit behind the wheel of a car, you must take certain preliminary instruction. Knowing where the brake is can be of considerable assistance when you have to make an emergency stop!

As with driving a car, or for that matter any other worthwhile pursuit, if you want to achieve success at giving presentations there is certain groundwork you must cover before you can even think about preparing and giving a presentation. It would be possible to omit this groundwork and simply give you a set of rules to follow. But without knowing *why* you would not always be able to apply the rules intelligently.

We will cover the groundwork first. Then we will go on to consider each stage in the process of preparing and giving a presentation.

CHAPTER 1

Basic Concepts

Let's start with the obvious question.

What is a presentation?

You may look on a presentation as being many things; an embarrassing experience, a chance to impress the boss, an entertainment. But whatever your view, it is likely to be coloured by your own feelings about having to stand up and face people. If you think of a presentation as some kind of personal trial, it is bound to affect your performance. The successful presenter takes an objective view.

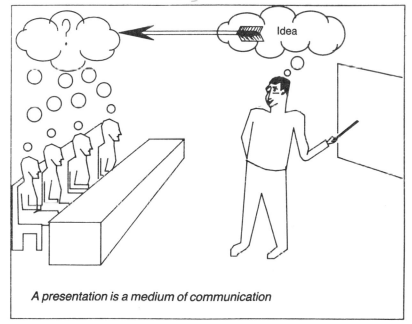

A presentation is a medium of communication

Figure 1.1

A presentation is a medium of communication

You have certain information which you wish to impart to your audience. Some of this information might be directly stated, 'the sales for the first quarter were . . . ', and some of this information might be transmitted in more subtle ways, by your behaviour, 'aren't I a clever so and so, and don't you think I should be promoted'.

It may be that the primary purpose of the presentation is to convey the stated facts. Or your principal concern might be for the audience to draw the right inferences. But whatever your purpose, the essential fact remains. *A presentation is a medium of communication.* And, if you want to be successful, never forget it.

. . . *Some communication is by more subtle means*

Figure 1.2

A successful presentation takes place when there is an efficient transfer of information from you to the audience

To be able to communicate effectively with the audience you need to understand something about the way in which the brain absorbs information. We will approach this from two angles. First we will look at the learning process, then we will cover memory. We will complete the discussion by using some examples to draw together the salient features of each topic.

The learning process

There are two main schools which attempt to explain the way in which the brain learns:

1. The Behaviourist school.
2. The Gestaltic school.

The Behaviourist school believes that learning takes place when the brain forms a connection between two events. You may have heard of the experiments carried out by Pavlov on dogs. In these experiments a dog is given a choice between taking one of two actions. If it takes the first action it is rewarded with food. If it takes the second action, it is punished. Within a short space of time the dog will learn to always select the first action. This theory is applied with success in the housetraining of domestic animals: give a dog a biscuit when he does it in the garden but whack him on the nose when he does it in the kitchen.

This type of behaviour is sometimes decribed as Stimulus–Response. The brain associates a given stimulus with a certain response. The behaviourist school believes that learning takes place when the brain starts to chain together a number of stimulus–response links.

The Gestaltic school believes that learning takes place through 'insight'. The learner will suddenly see a pattern which relates to other experiences. In seeing this pattern the information will be reorganised and a concept will be grasped.

Gestaltic theory is a little more difficult to come to terms with than the behaviourist theory. The best way to understand it is to find an example in your personal experience. There must have been a time when you were struggling to understand something which for a while just wouldn't sink in. Then, in a flash, everything became clear. The brain saw a pattern and the concept was understood. Another example of gestaltic theory supported by everyday life is the phrase, 'the penny dropped'.

Which one of these theories is correct? Neither of them, psychology is not an exact science. But both theories provide useful models that can be used to increase the effectiveness of the learning process (ie. increase the effectiveness of your presentation).

To be able to make good use of Gestaltic and Behaviourist theories, you must also understand something about the way people remember things.

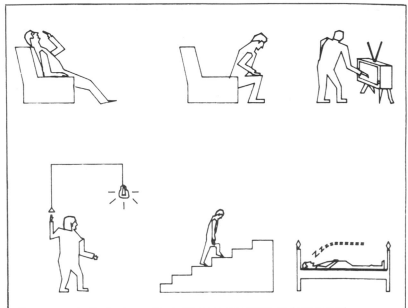

Some repeated behaviour patterns become automatic, and are a good example of Stimulus–Response type learning. The brain associates each action
with a following action. In the diagram above, Yawning is the 'Stimulus'. Getting out of the chair is the Response. Getting out of the chair also acts as the Stimulus for the next action, Switching off the T.V. This in turn will act as a Stimulus for the next action, and so on.

The complete process of going to bed can thus be viewed as a series of Stimulus–Response type links. This is what is meant by Stimulus–Response chaining.

Figure 1.3

Memory

The discussion on memory which follows shouldn't be regarded as clinically accurate. It presents a model which is valid for the purpose of designing a presentation.

Memory can be looked upon as operating on three separate levels:

1. Surface memory (seconds).
2. Short term memory (a few minutes to a couple of days).
3. Long term memory (many years).

At the surface memory level *everything* you see or hear is recorded,

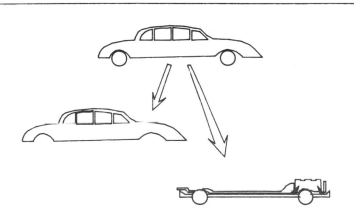

When you look at a car, you don't see a heap of metal and glass stuck together, you see a useful machine that gets you around. This way of looking at things corresponds with the Gestaltic theory, which states that we try to form patterns in the things we see. We try to collect things together and view them as an integrated whole.

This principle is illustrated further if you take the car apart in your mind. Instead of starting at one end and taking one bolt at a time, the natural way to proceed is to see the car as being made up of a series of sub-structures.

The brain likes to form patterns – logical structures, and will attempt to do so whenever it is presented with something new. This tendency to seek a structure can be harnessed to powerful effect when you are communicating with a group of people.

Figure 1.4

kept for a short period of time, and then wiped out (some of this information will be transferred to the short term memory before it is wiped out). As an illustration of this ability to retain a complete record over a short period, think of the occasion at school, when the teacher attempts to catch out a boy who is deeply engrossed in conversation with his friend. "Smith! What did I just say?" Smith looks up and, remarkably, recites the teacher's last sentence perfectly.

Had Smith been listening? No. At the time the teacher was speaking Smith was not even vaguely aware of what the teacher was saying. But the surface memory was working in the background soaking things up and rubbing things out. When Smith was asked to repeat what the teacher had said, he simply skimmed off the top of the surface memory buffer and regurgitated the teachers's words.

As the body's sensory input continually streams through the surface memory, the brain monitors the information, filtering out anything which it considers significant and transferring it to the short term memory. For an item to be considered significant it must 'stick out' in some way, for example:

The brain recognises an event which may affect survival (danger, food etc.).

It triggers an emotional response (a horrific accident, an attractive member of the opposite sex).

An event forms such a large proportion of the sensory input that it cannot be ignored (a big advertising board).

The intensity of an otherwise constant signal changes suddenly (a flash, a bang, or even sudden silence).

An event repeats itself (a flashing light).

The brain makes a concious effort to remember something.

The brain does not treat all these signals in an even way. For example, survival signals are given a much higher priority. Emotional signals are also given special treatment. In an extreme case an image which triggers a strong emotional response will be transferred directly to the *long term* memory (How often have you heard the phrase, 'I'll remember what I saw until the day I die'?).

The amount of information which can be transferred to the short term memory is limited in two ways. The rate at which new information can be received sets one limit; the capacity of the short term memory sets the other. In practice the capacity of the short term memory rarely presents a problem, but the *rate* at which information can be absorbed is a limiting factor, so care must be taken not to feed too much information in at once.

Once information is held in short term memory, it is available to the brain for processing. The brain uses the short term memory as a sort of working storage (the computer literate may wish to draw analogies between RAM and short term memory; disk storage and long term memory).

Each time the brain accesses information held in the short term memory, the brain will increase the significance rating of the record held (you could think of this as awarding points). Each time the 'significance rating' is increased, the period for which the information will be retained is extended. If no access is made to information within a short period of it being transferred to short term memory, it will be forgotten. If the brain accesses the information enough times then its 'significance rating' (total number of 'points' awarded) will cause it to be transferred to long term memory.

Another way that a piece of information could get an increased significance rating, would be if it was in some way reorganised. If the brain's filing system suddenly discovers that a piece of information should be cross-referenced to a number of other pieces of information, then its significance rating will increase markedly.

Why should the brain suddenly discover that one item of information should be cross-referenced with another? The brain will *always* try and find a pattern in any given set of information. This process will happen subconsciously, but will occasionally be given a 'boost' by conscious intervention (such as when solving puzzles).

When an item of information achieves significance because of its cross-references to other items, not only will the significance of the information increase, but the pattern of cross-references will be stored (think of it as a template). A pattern will require very little reinforcement before being transferred to long term memory.

The organisation of memory is illustrated in figures 1.5, 1.6 and 1.7.

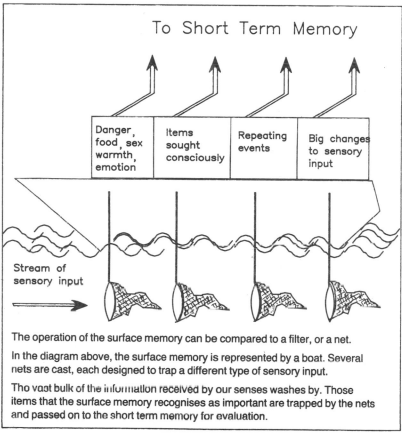

To Short Term Memory

| Danger, food, sex warmth, emotion | Items sought consciously | Repeating events | Big changes to sensory input |

Stream of sensory input

The operation of the surface memory can be compared to a filter, or a net.

In the diagram above, the surface memory is represented by a boat. Several nets are cast, each designed to trap a different type of sensory input.

The vast bulk of the information received by our senses washes by. Those items that the surface memory recognises as important are trapped by the nets and passed on to the short term memory for evaluation.

Figure 1.5

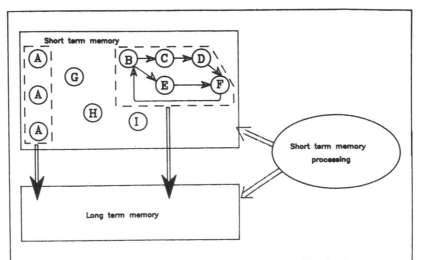

The brain constantly monitors the short term memory, looking for items that have been repeated and trying to establish patterns. In trying to see patterns the brain will compare information with that already held in the long term memory. If an item has been repeated, or if a pattern is recognised, the information achieves an increased significance rating. When the significance rating reaches a certain point, the information is transferred to long term memory.

In the diagram above, the brain has identified item A as a repeated item. Item A attains the required significance rating and is transferred to long term memory. Also, the brain has seen a pattern, a relationship connecting items B,C,D,E and F. This pattern attains a high significance rating, and the information is transferred to long term memory. Items G, H and I are not repeated, and no pattern is seen. These items will be quickly forgotten.

Figure 1.6

How do these ideas about memory fit in with the Behaviourist and Gestaltic theories of learning? Let's pretend to be school teachers and look at some examples.

You may know the nursery rhyme:

This is the cock that crowed in the morn,
that woke the priest all shaven and shorn,
that married the man all tattered and torn,
that kissed the maiden all forlorn,
that milked the cow with the crumpled horn,
that tossed the dog,
that chased the cat,
that killed the rat,

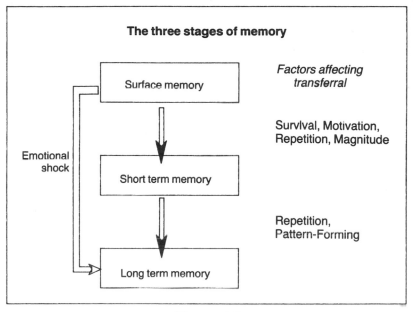

Figure 1.7

that ate the malt,
that lay in the house,
that Jack built.

If you were teaching this rhyme to a class of children, how would you go about it? The method that most of us would use instinctively is probably the best. To demonstrate this we will use the material covered above to derive a teaching approach.

The first step is to get the brain to recognise the information as significant and transfer it from surface memory into short term memory. You couldn't transfer the whole rhyme into short term memory, it's much too long. Or to put it another way the short term memory buffer would overflow. So you start off by getting the first line into short term memory. You do this by making sure that the brain recognises the information as significant. From the criteria outlined above, you could choose a number of ways of doing this, by *emphasising* the line (changing the intensity of the signal), by *repeating* it or by motivating the children to *make a conscious effort* to remember it. The safest way is to use all three methods, and most teachers would.

Once the line has been committed to short term memory, you have to make sure that it stays there, at least for the time being. You would start off by getting the children to repeat the line a few times, 'This is the cock that crowed in the morn'. When they had done that, you would say, 'This is the cock' and wait for the children to come back, 'that crowed in the morn'. In this way a stimulus–response link is created.

When the children have learned the first line, you teach them the second line. The phrase, 'that woke the priest,' would be the stimulus and 'all shaven and torn' would be the response. But do you ask them to recite the second line on its own? No. You get them to recite the first line followed by the second line. And then you would get them to say the first three lines.

In effect you are building up a pattern like this:

Stimulus[1]–Response[1]
Stimulus[1]–Response[1]–Stimulus[2]–Response[2]
Stimulus[1]–Response[1]–Stimulus[2]–Response[2]–Stimulus[3]–Response[3]

In teaching this nursery rhyme you are using the behaviourist theory of stimulus–response chaining. In the discussion on short term memory, we said that one of the ways for an item of information to gain permanence, was for the brain to continually re-access it. By making the children repeat the first line in each stage of the learning process, it becomes firmly imbedded in short term memory (and with repetition will eventually be transferred to long term memory). It is easy to access the first line, and once they have done that, the behaviourist 'links' take them to the other lines.

Let's take a Gestaltic example. Imagine that you are teaching a secondary school class on the theory of electrical circuits. You have defined the volt as a measure of electromotive force and said it represents a difference in potential. You have defined the ohm as a measure of resistance. You then introduce the amp, using Ohm's law, stating that the current is equal to the potential difference divided by the resistance: $I = V/R$. A sea of blank faces confronts you. How can you impart some kind of 'feel' for the subject you are trying to explain?

The problem here is very different to the nursery rhyme example given above. No amount of repetition or chaining of Stimulus–Response groups will help get the point across. We need to explain a concept, or to use the gestaltic term, we need to give the class 'insight'.

For Gestaltic learning to take place, the brain must be able to see a pattern. The best way to help the brain to see a pattern is to create some kind of model which the brain can compare with similar experiences. The easiest way to create a model is to use an analogy.

Consider the diagrams in figures 1.8 and 1.9.

Compare the electrical circuit to the water pump construction. The pump moves the water up into the high tank, giving it 'potential energy' proportional to the height, which is analogous to voltage. The pipe which carries the water has narrow turns in it, causing 'resistance' to the flow of the water, the greater the resistance, the slower the flow

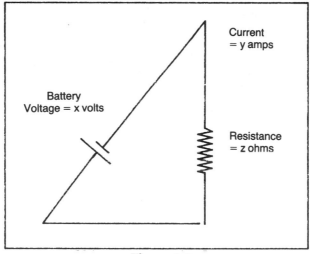

Figure 1.8

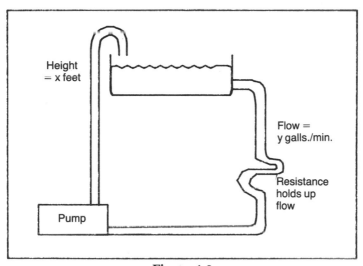

Figure 1.9

of water. The class will appreciate that the higher the tank, the faster will be the flow of the water. So we can say that the Current (flow of the water) is proportional to the potential (the height of the tank) and inversely proportional to the resistance (offered by the narrow bends in the pipe). Current = Potential/Resistance (choosing the right units). This is exactly the same formula which describes the electrical circuit.

As the class studies the water pump diagram, which they understand, they will draw parallels with the electrical circuit. Eventually they will see how the circuit works, or to put it another way, they will gain insight.

The learning process in this case has been Gestaltic. The class has developed a concept; an understanding of the whole. Will they remember it? With a little reinforcement of the point, yes. Because the information held by the brain has been reorganised into a pattern, cross-referencing water pumps with electrical currents. As we discussed above, when the brain reorganises information the significance rating increases, the information acquires a greater degree of permanence and it becomes more likely that it will be transferred to the long term memory.

Practical applications

What lessons can we learn from our discussion on learning and memory?

We will start off with a general point, because it deserves more importance than we have been able to give in the preceding section. Information will be transferred to the short term memory if the brain makes a conscious effort. This means: *Motivation is important.*

Information which triggers an emotional response is given high priority by the brain and will be assimilated automatically.

If we are putting a concept across it may be difficult to encourage the brain to see a pattern, but skilful use of analogy will often do the trick. Once the learner sees a pattern it will be grasped and remembered quite quickly. To put it another way, concepts are difficult to put across, but economical in terms of time.

If we are putting a series of facts across the best approach is to create a series of Stimulus–Response links and use repetition to drive the point home (motivation is very important here). This technique is easy to apply, but may require a lot of time. A continued barrage of facts is likely to overload the short term memory's capacity to receive information, leading to tiredness, frustration and de-motivation.

So far we have been going through some general ideas about learning. We will use the principles that we have established throughout the rest of this book.

In the next chapter we start to look specifically at the presentation medium and ask the question, 'When should we use a presentation?' And, more importantly, 'When should we avoid using a presentation?'

Read the summary on the next page before moving on.

Summary of chapter one – Basic concepts

What is a Presentation?

A medium of communication

The two schools of learning

Behaviourist — learn through making connections, associating reponses with stimuli. Ideas are learnt by chaining together Stimulus–
Response links.

Gestaltic — learn through forming patterns, by finding relationships
between items and combining them into an integrated whole.

Memory

Surface memory — acts as a filter, everything passes through, but only
important information is trapped for processing by the short term
memory.

Short term memory — recognises items as significant if they are
repeated or form patterns. Items receiving a high significance rating
will be transferred to long term memory.

Long term memory — holds information for many years.

Motivation to learn helps the memory processes.

Practical application

For facts use Stimulus–Response techniques — high repetition.

For concepts use Gestaltic techniques – form patterns and draw
analogies.

CHAPTER 2

Uses and Abuses

If you try to give a presentation, in circumstances where a presentation isn't called for, you will fail.

The presentation medium is excellent for certain uses. There is a tendency in large companies today to call for a presentation at the drop of a hat.

Do not look upon presentations as a panacea for all communication problems. If you abuse the medium it will cost you.

You may feel that you are the unwitting victim; always asked to give a presentation, and in no position to refuse. Don't panic, there are

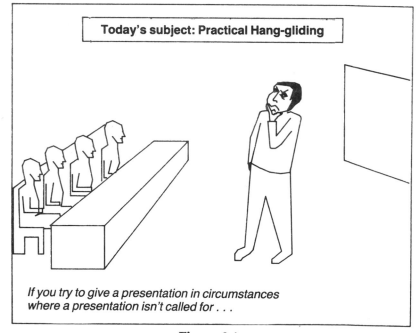

If you try to give a presentation in circumstances where a presentation isn't called for . . .

Figure 2.1

ways to give successful presentations, even when there is no real need. But such solutions require you to be aware that a problem exists.

In this chapter we will go through the disadvantages and advantages of presentations. We will use our findings to answer the question: When should a presentation be used? To conclude the chapter we examine the two main types of presentation and state the circumstances in which each type of presentation should be used.

Disadvantages of presentations

The disadvantages of the presentation medium fall into two categories; difficulties in dealing with certain types of subject matter, and those inherent in the medium itself. We will go through these difficulties, taking those associated with specific subjects first.

Subjects not suitable as presentation topics

Practical subjects cannot be taught using the presentation method as students can only develop practical skills by actually trying them out. A presentation could be used as a theory primer. Subjects with a limited practical content could be dealt with in a presentation if it is convenient to include a break to take care of the practical exercise.

Dry factual material does not come over well. In chapter one we showed that facts can be learned by creating stimulus–reponse links which are ingrained in the learner through constant repetition. This might be acceptable for the under fives, but wouldn't go down well in the commercial world!

To understand **complex, sociological issues** it is sometimes necessary for people to interact and learn through their own feelings and reactions. This sort of behaviour could well interrupt the presenter's concentration and may be considered improper in a business environment. Consequently, subjects of this nature are best avoided in presentations.

Interpersonal skills (such as selling, interviewing, dealing with staff)

Subject matter	Suggested alternative medium
Practical subjects	Practical workshop
Dry factual material	Reference booklet
Complex sociological subjects	Group sensitivity sessions
Interpersonal skills	Role play

Figure 2.2

cannot be taught at a theoretical level and are not suitable subjects for presentations. However, as with practical skills, it is quite usual to introduce these subjects by means of a presentation with more practical training to follow.

A summary of subjects not suitable as presentation topics is shown in figure 2.2, which also shows a suggested alternative medium.
Next, We will look at difficulties associated with the medium.

Difficulties of the presentation medium

A person sitting in a large audience can have a **feeling of isolation**. Because a large number of people are involved an individual may feel that it is an impersonal exercise, and, if the situation is not handled carefully, people will start to 'switch off'. Techniques for preventing a breakdown of attention are covered in chapter seven.
A presentation has **limited content**. In chapter one we stated that there is a limit on the rate at which the short term memory can absorb new facts. A consequence of this is that the amount of new information which the average person can absorb in a presentation is quite small. This difficulty cannot be overcome by using more time. Sessions which stretch for longer than an hour are likely to tire the brain to such a degree that less information can be learnt in a longer talk than could be learnt in a shorter talk (an economist might say that in a long talk the learner experiences marginal disutility).
A presentation has a **limited audience size** imposed by the physical constraints of the venue. A presentation to a large audience should, more properly, be regarded as a lecture. Nevertheless, we shall give some consideration to the problems of addressing large audiences later in this book.
Presentations have **high costs per person**. Setting up a presentation is expensive and relatively little information can be put across. This makes it an expensive medium if measured on a 'facts per buck' basis (especially if compared to the written medium, where a large amount of facts can be put together cheaply and distributed to an unlimited number of people).
Now that we've got the bad news out of the way, let's look at the advantages.

Advantages of presentations

The most important characteristic of a presentation is that it is **interactive**. Books may be a cheap way of transmitting information, but you cannot ask a book a question. And the book can't ask you a question to confirm that you've understood it correctly. Of course, there are other forms of learning which are also interactive; one-to-one tutorials, computer assisted learning; but none of these alternatives is as cheap or convenient as a presentation.

Because a presentation is interactive it can be **modified dynamically**. Or, to put it another way, the presentation you end up giving might be completely different from the one you set out to give. If you find out that the audience is particularly interested in one area, you can devote more time than you had planned to covering it and cut out a topic which is of less interest to the audience.

A presentation **addresses more than one sense**. Information is presented orally, and visually, through the written word and by means of diagrams. In the case of a subject such as geology, where rock samples might be passed around the audience, the tactile sense is involved. A talk on chemistry might include demonstrations where the senses of taste and smell are used. The more senses that are involved in the learning process, the better chance that the brain will receive the message. If ever you see an opportunity to get a point across by appealing to other than the usual auditory or visual senses, *use it!*

A presentation is **personal**. The information received by the audience is not limited to what you say or what you show them. A host of other signals are sent unconsciously by your body language.

One of the important pre-conditions for getting your point across is an atmosphere which is conducive to learning. The only way that you can ensure that the environment is correct is by being there.

Presentations are exceptionally **good for putting concepts across** using the Gestaltic type of learning which was covered in chapter one. Ideas can be introduced one at a time through several different senses and built upon to develop a principle. At each stage in the process the presenter can question the audience and identify and resolve areas of difficulty. Whenever a member of the audience has trouble following the logic of the argument, the presenter can be stopped and questioned.

Persuasive arguments can be put very effectively through a presentation. For example, if you are trying to convince other members of your company that a certain course of action should be followed, a presentation is a most effective way of impressing your opinion on them. The effectiveness of a persuasive argument can depend to a large extent on the way the talk is structured. we will cover this in chapter four.

During a presentation you have a **psychological advantage** because you control the environment. By presenting your case personally to your colleagues you have their involvement. And with that goes their commitment. If you really want to drive an advantage home, try to force a collective decision *at your presentation*. (The author is not recommending railroading your colleagues as a preferred management technique. The intention is to illustrate the persuasive power of a good presentation. How you use it is up to you!)

A presentation can be **entertaining**. For learning to be effective it is important to relieve tension occasionally by introducing humour. A group of people can interact to create a cheerful atmosphere. (Of course there is a danger that this can be over done. You may well have been on courses which were very entertaining, but you can't actually remember learning anything.)

Now that we know the advantages and disadvantages of the presentation medium, we are in a position to answer the next question.

When should a presentation be used?

At the beginning of this book we stated that a presentation was a medium of communication. Like all media of communication it is best suited to certain purposes.

To repeat the statement made at the beginning of this chapter:

If you try to give a presentation, in circumstances where a presentation isn't called for, you will fail.

Let's take an obvious example. Your department has been given new telephones which enable your staff to call major customers by using a three digit short code. Do you use a presentation to teach them the short codes? Of course not. But you will often find that some people will give a presentation comprising facts as dry as phone numbers.

You might be saying to yourself, 'But what if my boss has *told* me to give a presentation. Telling him that it's an inappropriate medium isn't likely to get me any brownie points.'

If you are asked to give a presentation, you set your objective so that the circumstances *do* call for a presentation. This needn't create difficulties. To take an obvious example, if you had been asked to talk about hang-gliding your objective will be to teach the theory of hang-gliding, and not to teach the audience how to hang-glide. Not much of a difference in the way the objective is phrased, but it has dramatic implications on your approach to the presentation. We will deal with objectives in some depth later on in the book.

Our review of advantages and disadvantages has already highlighted some areas where a presentation shouldn't be used; for putting over practical subjects, dry facts, complex sociological issues, interpersonal skills. We have also noted that presentations are especially good for putting over concepts or persuasive arguments.

Presentations can be used to instruct, to persuade or to inform. They should *not* be used to entertain (although they should be entertaining). They should *not* be used because 'everyone else is giving one'. They should *not* be used to impress the boss. Don't give a presentation unless you have something useful to say. If you have been asked to give a presentation, *find* something useful to say. We will deal with this at considerable length in the next chapter.

Before committing yourself to a presentation, there are a number of practical constraints which you should consider.

Have you got adequate time to prepare? If you are inexperienced it will take well over a day to prepare an hour's presentation. To do a good job on your first presentation three or four days is not an unreasonable amount of time.

How many people do you need to inform? A presentation given to ten people is ideal. You *can* address as many as you can fit into a room. *But the degree of difficulty in communicating increases dramatically as the number of people increases beyond fifteen.* If large numbers of people are involved, you should consider breaking them up into small groups, or communicate using a different medium.

Can you get hold of all the equipment you need? An obvious point which is often overlooked. We will deal with preparation again in chapter seven.

Can you afford the cost? Your time is expensive and so is that of your audience (you might be depleting an entire office while you are talking to them). If you are sure that you have something useful to say costs will usually be justifiable, but it is a factor worth considering if budgets are tight.

Can your intended audience get time off to listen to you? Don't find out after spending two days of preparation.

If you have decided that a presentation is the appropriate medium for the job in hand, there is still one more decision to be made, before you can start thinking about the talk itself.

What type of talk should it be?

Most presentations fall between two extremes: the lecture type of talk, where the presenter dominates and little interaction takes place; and the discussion type of talk where the presenter sits among the audience and gives a general direction to the conversation. (You could also classify talks in other ways, for example slide shows and blackboard-based, but these sort of differences will be covered in the chapter on visual aids.)

In general, learning is more effective in an interactive environment. *But you must be able to retain effective control.* If the audience gets the upper hand then you will lose credibility and no information will be transmitted.

Your talk will come somewhere between the lecture style and the discussion style. Several factors will determine whether you lean more towards one way or the other.

Most presentations fall between extremes . . .

Figure 2.3

If you are keen to find out what the audience *really* think about something, a cosy, conversational atmosphere will help to reduce their inhibitions. Take them in small groups and conduct the presentation as naturally as possible. You can conduct a presentation of this type from a seated position, but you must be extremely confident of your ability to control the group if you are to do this.

If you are bringing controversial news which is likely to have the audience in uproar, and you are fearful of the situation degenerating into a squalid argument: keep things very formal. Set the tone and make sure you have firm control before letting the cat out of the bag.

The relationship between you and the audience prior to the presentation will also affect the style of the talk.

If you are going to be talking to a group of people who are senior to you, an informal presentation is ill-advised. If you try and address senior people, by 'coming down' to their level, their natural superiority will quickly emerge. When you are giving the presentation, you must control the room. If you stand up and present formally, you will achieve that control automatically.

Conversely, if you are addressing staff who are junior to you, they will already feel intimidated to a certain degree. A relaxed atmosphere will help remove psychological barriers between you and the audience.

To summarise:

  Use a formal lecture-type talk when you are concerned about retaining control, typically when addressing a hostile audience or speaking to senior management.

  Use a relaxed discussion-type talk when you want to reduce inhibitions, typically if you want to hear their views or if you are addressing junior staff.

Summary of chapter two — Uses and abuses

Disadvantages of presentations

Not suitable for practical subjects, straight facts, interpersonal skills or complex sociological subjects requiring the audience to interact.

Tendency for members of audience to feel remote.

Limited as to time and the amount of information which can be covered.

The number of people which can be addressed is limited.

Costly on a 'facts per buck' basis.

Advantages of presentations

Interactive.

Can be modified dynamically ('in flight').

Addresses more than one sense.

Personal ('body-language' between presenter and audience)

Good for concepts and persuasive arguments.

Presenter has control over the learning environment.

Group interaction facilitates the introduction of humour to relieve tension.

When should a presentation be used?

To instruct, to persuade or to inform.

But only when you have something worth saying.

When time, cost, space, equipment and availability constraints have been checked.

What type of talk should be used?

Lecture-type to maintain control and for senior managers.

Discussion type to reduce inhibitions and for junior staff.

CHAPTER 3

Subject Matter and Content

In chapter one we covered some basic theory. From chapter two you know in which circumstances you should use a presentation, and which type of presentation is likely to be appropriate. Throughout the rest of this book we are going to go through the stages involved in preparing and giving a presentation.

The first problem that confronts the aspiring presenter is pretty basic. What is going to be the subject of the presentation? You already have some idea about what is likely to be a good topic for a presentation, from the material covered in chapter two. But as yet the guidelines we have set in this area have been very broad. In this chapter we will discuss the subject matter in depth.

When you give a talk, you may be left free to decide upon your own topic or, more often, be given a subject which you are expected to cover.

If you are given choice of subject matter you will first have to pick the broad area to be covered and then decide upon the detailed content of the talk. In cases where you are asked to talk about a given subject your decision will be limited to setting the detailed points to be included in the presentation.

We will first look at the considerations involved in choosing the subject matter and then extend these principles to look at how you would decide upon the detailed content of a presentation.

Picking a subject

There are two main limitations to your choice of subject matter:

1. The audience
2. The amount of time available

To illustrate the importance of correctly assessing the audience think of an extreme example. Would you book a northern club comedian to talk to the local women's church social? Not unless you were very naive or being deliberately mischievous.

22

The example is obvious. But the principle is important and the danger is usually far more subtly disguised. You must think carefully about the type of people you are addressing. What are their interests? What are their needs? It is easy to fall into the assumption that subjects which you find interesting appeal in the same way to other people. Sometimes choosing the wrong subject could be disastrous (for example a keen huntsman unwittingly addressing a group containing a large number of animal rights supporters).

The first point we could make is: Avoid anything controversial.

Try to be positive and find a subject which you know they will *want* to find out about. When you have the choice, picking an inherently interesting subject is a lot easier than trying to breathe life into something dull. Alternatively, pick something that might be *unexpectedly* interesting. Bringing out surprising new facts on an otherwise ordinary topic is often effective.

Our next point: Be imaginative and address yourself to the interests *of the audience.*

When you have thought about the audience, look at the time constraints.

One of the commonest mistakes made by inexperienced speakers is that they try to say too much. Seasoned parliamentarians often speak for ten or fifteen minutes making a point that could be summed up in one short sentence. On technical subjects you may need much longer than this to get something over effectively. The theory of relativity would not be a suitable subject for a ten minute spot!

Concepts which seem straightforward to you may have been assimilated over a long period of time. When you start to analyse a subject and break it down, you may find that to make a fairly basic point you need to introduce a whole series of underlying facts to lay the groundwork. Worse, you may give the presentation and suddenly be confronted by a battery of questions on 'obvious' points. Never underestimate your own capacity to make assumptions. (You may have heard the old joke, never assume — it makes an ass of u and me).

To summarise: Don't be too ambitious in your choice of subject. You must take time to make a point if you want to make it well.

We have been considering the case where you have been able to choose the subject of a presentation. Of course, in practice you are more likely to be told what you should talk about. In either event setting the scope of the talk will almost certainly be down to you.

Setting the scope of the presentation

We said in the last section that, where you have a choice, you should talk on a subject which is inherently interesting. In this section we will find out how to *make* a subject interesting.

In chapter two we said that before you give a talk you must have something worthwhile to say. Another way of putting this is: You must have a message. Whatever limitations are placed on the subject matter the **message** you get across is up to you. *Deciding on the message is the most crucial part of your preparation.* Let us explore further what we mean by the 'message'.

The subject of your talk is likely to be loosely defined. For instance, senior management have asked you to do a short talk on the new purchase order system. After months spent wrestling with the technicalities of the new system you are desperate to show someone how clever you are, laying bare the complexities, showing how you solved the problems.

You decide to plan out the talk in a logical, structured way: state what the inputs to the system are, explain what processing is involved, describe the hardware and state the outputs of the system.

You might think that a talk like this would be a fair response to the request, and perhaps in a perfect world it would. But a presentation along these lines would be at best boring and at worst disastrous.

Why? Because you haven't addressed the interests of the audience. *And you haven't got a message.*

When we looked at short term memory in chapter one, we noted that information which triggers an emotional response is given a high priority. The essence of a good message is that it will trigger an emotional response. You may wonder if it is possible for a message to appeal to the emotions and still have commercial relevance. *People are emotionally involved in their jobs.* If they feel deeply about something it is likely to be because it has commercial relevance. It may be that they feel deeply about the wrong things. If so, that is a point you should address in your presentation.

When you are thinking about the subject matter, ask yourself, what are their interests? What do they *want* to know? What do they *care* about? Senior managers worry about profitability, customer relations, implications for future growth. These are the areas you must address.

Once you have targeted the right area, decide on the message.

The purchase order system will reduce costs.
The purchase order system will improve customer relations.
The purchase order system has little capacity for growth.

Any of these could be the message.

Trainee salesmen are taught to sell *benefits* not *features*. In the same way a good message should concentrate on information which the audience finds beneficial, not features which you find interesting.

What is the most important thing about the message? *The message must address the interests of the audience.*

Today's subject: Courtship etiquette

The message must address the interests of the audience . . .

Figure 3.1

A good message will have other qualities.

1. It will be short and to the point.
2. It will affect people's behaviour after they have left the room.

We will look at each of these points in turn.

A short clear message is easy to understand and easy to remember. The benefits of a short message have long been recognised by the advertising business. How many times have you heard a snappy slogan used to sell a product? Your audience will feel happy if they are given material which is easily digestible. Condensing what you have to say into a few short statements will give the audience something which is easy to understand and easy to take away with them. Of course, our intention is that the audience takes away rather more than one simple message. The message is the focus which brings all the other points together.

But what do we mean when we say that a good message should affect people's behaviour after they have left the room? Isn't this the same thing as saying it should be easy to remember? No. Consider the message:

You will appreciate the difficulties of assessing credit ratings

The message is reasonably short and to the point and, assuming the audience is composed of accountants, addresses their interests. But it doesn't give them anything concrete. A good message should contain something of practical value. Consider the following:

There are three simple ways to reduce your exposure to bad debts. After this talk you will know them and be able to apply them.

Compared to the previous example the message is quite long. But it is infinitely superior. There is a solid practical benefit to be gained from the presentation.

To summarise:

For a talk to be successful it must have a message which addresses the interest of the audience, is short and to the point and has solid practical value.

The message is what puts the fire into the belly of the talk. It embodies the whole thrust of the presentation.

Let's take stock and look at how far we have come in preparing a presentation.

You have decided on the subject matter and have put a lot of careful thought into finding the *right* message for the audience.

You cannot put too much time into thinking about the right message.

Your thoughts on the message may well have modified your ideas on the subject matter. Now is the time to set a General Objective for the presentation.

A General Objective is a title that the audience can relate to. It is significant in that it frames the audience's expectations. Do not give away the message in the general objective. The message is your trump card; hold it back and play it to gain maximum effect.

For example, if you have been asked to give a presentation on the new purchase order system inform the attendees that the object of the talk is 'to give an understanding of the impact of the system on the rest of the business'. This statement is the general objective. Wait until you have them in front of you before giving them the message; then you can give it with punch.

It may seem a backward way of doing things to come up with a general objective after deciding on a message, but there is good reason for doing it this way. Deciding upon a message forces you to look at things from the audience's point of view and clarifies what the thrust of the presentation is going to be. After going through this process you are more likely to come up with a valid general objective.

The important thing to remember when you are setting a general

Figure 3.2

objective is that the audience will look at the title of your talk and auto-matically form a series of assumptions and preconceptions. Use this to your advantage by getting the audience to think on the right wavelength.

In the example above we said that that the general objective was 'understanding the impact on the business ... '. This statement in no way detracts from the effectiveness of a punchy message, but it does get the audience thinking along the right lines. If you had set the title of the talk as 'The purchase order system' and left it at that, the audience would be unsure what to expect. It is an important balance to strike, creating the right sort of expectations, but holding back on the attention-grabbing message.

Later, when we look at the techniques of presentation, we will find out that creating expectations and then confirming them to be correct is an important psychological tool in promoting effective learning. For the time being think of the way the professional comedian times things, he will create a situation where something is bound to happen and then, just as you can 'see it coming', he delivers the punchline. The joke is made much funnier because the skilful comic creates expectations and then confirms and reinforces them.

We have now got to the stage of preparation where you have written down a Message and a General Objective. The next step is to start planning out the talk in detail. But before you go on to the next chapter read through the summary on the next page.

Summary of chapter three – Subject matter and content

Picking a subject

Assess the audience

    Avoid anything controversial.

    Be imaginative and address the interests *of the audience*.

Look at the time constraints

    Don't be too ambitious in your choice of subject. You must, take
    time to make a point if you want to make it well.

Setting the scope of the presentation

Decide upon a central Message which must:

    address the interests of the audience.

    be short and to the point.

    have solid, practical value.

Set a General Objective which will:

    be a title which the audience can relate to.

    avoid stealing the thunder of the message.

    create the right expectations in the audience.

CHAPTER 4

Structure

In the stages of preparation we have looked at so far, we have covered how to decide on a punchy Message and pick a suitable General Objective.

Equally important as the Message, is the way you put it over. And the most crucial factor affecting the success you achieve in putting over the message is the *structure*.

In this chapter you will find out how to build a skeleton for a talk. First we will ask, why do we need a structure? Then we will look at the preparation for structuring, and finally we will find out how the structure of the talk is set.

Why do we need a structure?

In the discussion on Gestaltic learning in chapter one, we stated that the brain, when confronted with any new items of information, will instinctively try and form a pattern. When you give a presentation to an audience, they will, on a subconscious level, constantly compare and sort the different things that you say, trying to arrange the facts presented into some kind of logical order.

If an audience is not able to find a logical cohesion in your presentation, they will be dissatisfied. They may not know why they are dissatisfied, but they will feel distinctly uneasy. To avoid this happening there are two things you must do:

1. Structure your talk in a logical way.
2. Tell your audience what the structure is at the beginning of the talk.

Why do you need to spell out the structure at the beginning of the talk? Because it helps the brain considerably if it has an idea of what kind of pattern is to be created. When you spell out the structure, the brain creates an empty framework. As the new information comes along, the brain slots each item into the spaces waiting in the framework. Make sure that the brain creates a pattern, and you make sure that the information you present has a solid footing in the short term memory.

Another good reason for presenting the structure 'up front' has already been touched upon in chapter three. If you create an expectation, and then confirm it to be correct, you give a small boost to the audience's ego. This stimulates motivation and enhances the learning process.

Now that you know *why* 'structure is important, let's find out *how* to start designing a structure.

Preparing to structure your talk

What must you do before you can work out a structure?

1. Define what you wish to achieve.
2. Distinguish between what you must explain, and what the audience already know.

For the moment we will concentrate on defining what you wish to achieve. There is only one way to do this properly. You must set Specific Objectives.

Before we define a Specific Objective, let us recall something which was stated in chapter three. We said that a talk must have a Message. We also said that a message must have solid practical value. To put it another way, when your listeners leave the room they must be able to do something they couldn't do before.

A Specific Objective states in precise terms something which the listener will be able to do as a result of attending your presentation.

Professional trainers place a great amount of importance on specific objectives. To understand why they are so important it is necessary to know how a trainer defines learning.

Learning can be said to have taken place when a measurable change in behaviour is observed.

Let's look a little closer at this statement.

If a trainee is given instruction, and no change in behaviour takes place, then you could say that the instruction has accomplished nothing. How can you tell if a change in behaviour has taken place? By subjecting the trainee to a test.

For example, if the object of the instruction is to teach the trainee the name of the capital of France, one could ascertain a change in behaviour as follows:

Before the instruction, ask the trainee, 'What is the capital of France?'

Note the response — a blank look.

After the instruction, ask the trainee, 'What is the capital of France?' Note the response — 'Paris'.

Of course, in a commercial environment you will not always want to test your listeners at the end of a presentation. Your senior managers might object if, at the end of a sales report, they were given pencils, rubbers and examination papers! But if the purpose of your presentation is to instruct (for example teaching junior staff how to use a new system), you should always test.

Having defined learning as a change in behaviour, we could say that a Specific Objective is a precise description of the behaviour that we are trying to instill in the trainee. That is why, in training circles, Specific Objectives are referred to as Behavioural Objectives.

Because a change in behaviour is *precise* and *measurable*, there are certain things we could say about Specific (Behavioural) Objectives.

A Specific Objective must spell out in very clear terms exactly what it is that the trainee will be able to do.

A Specific Objective must refer to an action which is observable.

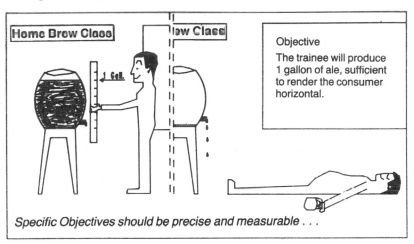

Specific Objectives should be precise and measurable . . .

Figure 4.1

For example, 'The trainee will understand the concepts of Operating Systems', is not a valid Specific Objective because it is neither precise or measurable.

'The trainee will be able to talk about operating systems', is not a valid Specific Objective. It is measurable (we can record what he says), but it is not precise.

'The trainee will be able to count to twenty, in his head, within half a second', is not a valid Specific Objective because it is precise but not measurable.

'The trainee will be able to discriminate between chalk and cheese', is a good Specific Objective because it is both precise and measurable.

Formal books on training will further define Specific Objectives by stating that they should contain conditions and standards. This approach is a strong part of training in the armed services, where objectives are likely to read something like this:

> Given access to a standard tool kit, in a well-ventilated room of normal temperature, the trainee will be able to join two pieces of metal of thickness between 0.5mm and 0.7mm. The joint will be watertight and to a tolerance of 0.001mm.

This Objective has conditions, 'Given access to a standard tool kit, in a well-ventilated room of normal temperature', and standards, 'the joint being watertight and to a tolerance of 0.001mm'. For the purposes of giving presentations in a commercial environment you do not need to define your objectives anything like as precisely as this. But it is illuminating to be aware that some instructors go to such trouble.

When you set objectives for your presentation, there are two hints that will help you set valid Specific Objectives

1. Avoid the words, 'understand' and 'appreciate'.
2. When you have phrased the objective, precede it with the words 'watch me'. If it doesn't make sense it is unlikely to be a valid objective ('Watch me list . . . ' is ok but 'Watch me understand . . .' is nonsensical).

How do you decide what your Specific Objectives should be? They will be whatever is necessary to put over your Message.

Ask yourself the question, 'What will the audience be able to do at the end of the presentation?' Then list out the Specific Objectives.

Let's take an example. You have been asked to talk to senior management about the new purchase order system. The message is, 'The purchase order system will reduce costs by ten thousand pounds'. The General Objective for the talk is, 'to give the audience an appreciation of the cost benefits of the new system'.

You must decide what you want the audience to be able to do when they leave the room. Remember that the audience is comprised of potential ambassadors for your new system. It's not just a question of giving them warm feelings, they must be able to put over your message and back it up.

Your first list of Specific Objectives might resemble that which follows.

The trainee will be able to:

List the areas in which cost cuttings will be achieved.
State the amount of saving that will be achieved in each area.
Explain how the system will lead to lower stock levels.
Explain how the system will improve cash flow.
Compare the labour requirements and costs for the old and new
   systems.

When you have made a list of Specific Objectives, there is one more
thing you should do before working out the strucuture of the talk.

We said at the beginning of this section that before you can structure
a talk you must define what you wish to achieve and distinguish
between what you must explain and what the audience already know.
We have spent some time looking at how you should define what you
wish to achieve. But the second part of the statement is no less
important.

If you are going to be talking in a commercial environment it is
almost inevitable that when you give a talk you will assume the
audience to have some degree of specialised knowledge. There is often
a danger that you will assume too much.

In chapter three, we said that you should assess the audience
carefully before deciding on a Message, to ensure that the Message
addressed their interests. Another good reason for assessing the
audience is that it enables you to set Prerequisites.

When you have finished writing down your Specific Objectives,
look at them carefully and ask the question, 'What does the audience
need to know before they can understand this?'

Write down the answer to this question. It is your list of prerequisites.

When you have written down your prerequisites, consider the
audience again. Do they fit the bill? This isn't the kind of question that
can be glossed over lightly. If you've got a collection of people who
have given up valuable time to listen to you, and they can't understand
half of what you're saying — You've got trouble on your hands.

If there are discrepancies between your list of prerequisites and the
knowledge of the audience, you must change something. Either you
cover the necessary background information in the talk, or you change
your objectives.

To continue with the example of the talk on the purchase order
system, an example list of prerequisites follows.

The audience will:

have knowledge of accounting techniques and concepts.
be familiar with the existing systems of the company.
be familiar with basic concepts of data processing.

Checking the prerequisites is very important when you wish to use a

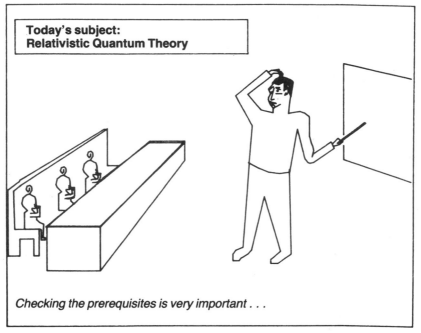

Figure 4.2

talk for the second time. For example, the presentation about the purchase order system might be a great success, when given to senior management, but would be a disaster if repeated to a group of engineers with no accounting knowledge. A disciplined approach to setting prerequisites will ensure that this kind of mistake never happens.

How precisely should you set prerequisites? In the example above, where the talk is to be given to members of your own company, a rough specification is sufficient. If you were giving a talk to strangers, however, the prerequisites should be used as a pre-condition for attendance at your presentation, and they should be spelt out in much greater detail.

When you have a list of Specific Objectives and Prerequisites, you can start to map out the structure of the talk.

Setting the structure

The overall structure of the talk will depend, to a certain extent, on the purpose of the presentation. There are three major types of structure which have proved effective for different purposes. We will look at each of these in turn.

The Scientific form:

    Purpose of study
    Method adopted
    Data
    Interpretation
    Conclusion

The Scientific form is most commonly used in the academic world, where the pattern of work is normally a period gathering data, followed by a period of evaluation. In the commercial world it can be used to present an *impartial* assessment of some kind of study. Examples of possible uses are, presenting the results of market research, interpreting a survey of staff attitudes. The talk may conclude with a firm conclusion, present a number of equally valid conclusions, or may even be open ended, in effect concluding that no conclusion is possible. In a commercial environment you would be strongly advised to avoid an open ended conclusion (especially if money has been invested in the research).

The Persuasive form:

    State proposed course of action
    Go through reasons against
    Demolish reasons against
    Go through reasons for
    Summarise reasons for
    Conclusion

Use the Persuausive form to deliver a *prejudiced* argument supporting a course of action. The audience will be in no doubt as to the preferred course of action. The danger with this sort of structure is that you may go over the top and the audience will dismiss your arguments as being irrationally biased. The most effective persuasive presentations are constructed with a great degree of subtlety. Try and arrange things so that the audience weigh the facts and feel as if *they* make the decision.

The Classical form

    Outline
    Stage one
    Recap stage one
    Stage two
    Recap stages one and two
    Stage three
    Recap stages one, two and three
    Conclusion

The Classical form is used for any Presentation which doesn't require one of the other two forms described above, that is for an instructive or an informative presentation. The talk doesn't *have* to be in three parts, but experience shows that people like things to be structured in threes, so if a you can arrange for a subject to be presented in three sections, so much the better.

Mapping out the structure

When you have decided on the overall structure, you can map out the content of the talk. The best way to do this, is to form a hierarchical structure, with the Message at the top. Underneath the message, group your Specific Objectives, with major objectives at the top and subordinate objectives at the bottom.
The precise way in which the Objectives are grouped will depend on the structure you are using. (You may feel that the objectives will not always fall into groupings which are consistent with the structures outlined above, but in practice you will find that for persuasive or scientific talks the objectives fall naturally into the categories required. With experience, you will find yourself formulating objectives with the structure of the talk in mind.)
The structure for a talk in the Classical style, which is in three parts is shown in figure 4.3.

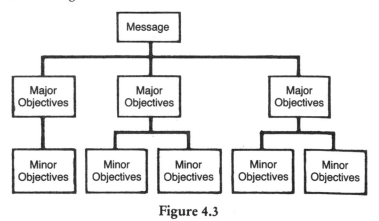

Figure 4.3

The process of structuring presents an interesting dilemma. In our discussions on learning we said that presentations are good for concepts and bad for straightforward facts. But in this chapter we have been concentrating on reducing the talk to a small set of narrowly defined objectives, if you like, arranging the presentation into a stream of easily stated facts.

How can these approaches be reconciled? The key lies in two words, *relevance* and *relation*. By structuring downwards from your message, you automatically ensure that what you have to say is relevant. And the very process of structuring creates relationships.

What is a *concept*? The Shorter Oxford Dictionary defines a concept as, 'an idea of a class of objects, a general notion', citing as an example the statement by Sir W. Hamilton, 'Concepts are merely the results, rendered permanent by language, of a previous process of comparison'.

In terms of our discussion on Gestaltic learning, you could say that the 'pattern' which the brain searches for in a given set of facts is a concept.

So how do we teach a concept? By introducing a series of facts, and then highlighting the relationship between them, helping the brain to go through the 'process of comparison' referred to by Sir W. Hamilton.

So the process is:

facts + pattern = concept

You might like to think of this as:

Specific Objectives + Structure = Message

We will finish off the chapter by completing the example of the purchase order talk. The structure is shown in the example in figure 4.4. Each box contains a statement of fact which corresponds to a Specific Objective (compare with the list of Specific Objectives on page 33).

The Message and Objectives for this example may not seem very 'conceptual', but, as we explained above, concepts are derived from relationships between facts. The purchase order talk revolves very much around relationships.

The purchase order system will save money *because* there is a saving of two thousand on stocks, three thousand on cash flow and five thousand on labour. There is a saving of two thousand on stocks *because* there is a link to the stock system and a trigger mechanism.

The word *because* signifies a causal relationship. Concepts are built from relationships.

If you have trouble in structuring a talk because you cannot relate facts together properly; it means that you are trying to introduce something which is irrelevant. Waste no time in striking it off your agenda!

Sometimes you may have trouble with sequencing. Point A cannot be covered until point B has been explained. But point B cannot be covered until point A has been explained! If this problem occurs it usually means that you have left something out. Inserting a section which covers a basic principle common to both points A and B will solve the problem.

Don't be afraid to revise your list of Specific Objectives. Often, it is only through the discipline of structuring that you become aware of your own unconscious assumptions and woolly thinking. Don't try to butcher the structure to make up for your earlier deficiencies; recognise them for what they are and take action to correct.

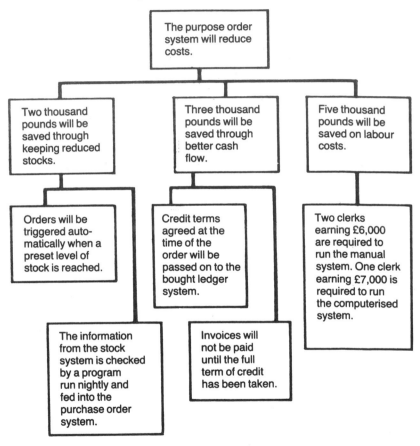

Figure 4.4

Summary of chapter 4 – Structure

Why do we need structure?
To help the brain establish a pattern and facilitate the learning process (Gestaltic theory of learning).

To create expectations which are subsequently verified, thus motivating the audience.

Preparing to structure your talk

Define what you wish to achieve in terms of *Specific Objectives* which state in precise, practical terms what the audience will be able to do as a result of listening to your presentation (Behavioural Objectives).

Distinguish between what you must explain, and what the audience already know. Set prerequisites for attending the talk and make sure that the audience meets your prerequisites.

Reassess your Objectives in the light of the prerequisites.

Setting the structure

Choose the right form of structure (scientific, persuasive or classical) for your purpose.

Construct a hierarchical tree of points, consistent with the form of your talk, with the message at the top. Each point should correspond with a Specific Objective. Remember that everything must be *relevant* and logically *related*.

Revise your Objectives as necessary.

CHAPTER 5

Use of Aids

Once you have mapped out a structure, it is time to start constructing the detailed material for the presentation. There are two things that must be done: preparing your aids and writing your notes. In this chapter we will deal with aids.

Do you need to use aids? Unequivocally — Yes.

Studies have shown that knowledge is absorbed through a combination of all the senses. The percentage of knowledge input through each sense is roughly as follows:

Vision	75%
Hearing	13%
Feeling	6%
Smelling	3%
Tasting	3%

It is not necessary to go to great lengths in interpreting these results; the message comes over loud and clear. *The visual sense plays an extremely important part in learning.*

It is no surprise to find that visual images are so important. After all, the brain was not 'designed' to communicate through language which was an ingenious, if inevitable, development. Early man communicated with his environment through images and feelings.

If you have any doubt about the power of the visual sense, think of your favourite films. Now think of the most memorable lines in those films. How many lines can you remember? Not many. Now try to think of the most memorable images. They come flooding to the top of the mind; Bogart with the drooping cigarette in Casablanca, O'Toole riding out of the desert in Laurence of Arabia, or even Darth Vader poised over Sir Alec Guinness in Star Wars.

It is also true that instances are best remembered when experienced through a combination of the senses. Do you have any idyllic memories of youth? A summer's day, a beautiful landscape, the scent of wild flowers, the soft chirping of birds, the warmth of the sun on your skin; it all becomes more alive, *and more memorable* as more senses are involved.

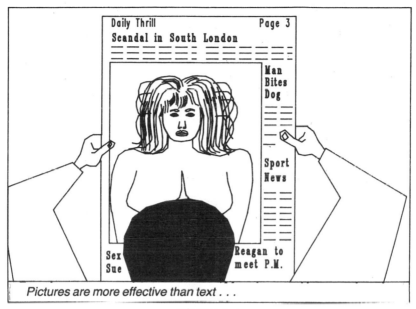

Figure 5.1

There is an old Chinese saying:

I hear and I forget
I see and I remember
I do and I understand

Remember this saying and it will serve you well. It highlights, not only the importance of visual aids, but reminds of the importance of audience participation as well. There will be more discussion on the need for audience participation in the next chapter.

Knowing that aids are important is not enough. We need to know the various types of aids which are available, when they should be used, how to decide which aids are appropriate and how to make them up. In this chapter we will address all these questions. Later on in the book you will learn how to present your aids effectively.

We will start by looking at types of aids, highlighting the advantages and disadvantages of each.

Blackboard/Whiteboard

The blackboard is the best known aid being familiar from school days. In the form of its modern replacement, the white board(with special pens and cleaner) it still retains popularity in the commercial world.

Disadvantages:

No more than one board of information can be prepared in advance.
Material is lost at the end of the presentation.
Writing on the board is time consuming (especially if pictures are involved).
The presenter must turn away from the audience.
Blackboards can create a lot of dust. Whiteboards (especially water based) can be very messy.
Quality of image often substandard as it depends on the skill of the presenter.

Advantages:

Extremely flexible.
Big pictures possible.
Ideal for altering/adapting an image as the presentation progresses.
Good for interactive sessions. Audience comments/responses can be listed on the board and dealt with in turn.
Places no constraints on the way the presentation develops.

Flipcharts

Flipcharts are widely available in most commercial organisations, and are the cheapest form of visual aid available.

Disadvantages

Limited to the size of paper available.
Material cannot be erased/altered.
If material is not prepared in advance, writing on the chart is time consuming.
The presenter must turn away from the audience to write on the chart.
Quality of image often substandard as it depends on the skill of the presenter.
Quality of paper and image will deteriorate after a few uses.

Advantages

Flexible.
Cheap.
Portable.
Can be prepared in advance (tip: to impress an audience prepare your work in light pencil — the audience will not be able to see it. You can then astound them with your amazing memory and arithmetic ability as you go over the light pencil markings with a

felt tipped marker pen).

Useful for interactive sessions. Audience comments/responses can be listed on the chart and dealt with (but not so good as using corner of black/whiteboard as flipchart must be flipped over and back to retrieve points).

Places no constraints on the way the presentation develops.

Magnetic/felt boards

Good for specialised uses but not widely available. Not as flexible or easy to use as black/white boards or flipcharts and will not be considered further here.

Overhead projector

Probably the most commonly used visual aid in in commerce.

Disadvantages

Requires electricity supply.

Bulbs prone to fail at crucial moment in presentation.

Takes time to set up and adjust.

Requires time to prepare slides.

Cannot be used for highly detailed diagrams or photographs.

Sometimes noisy and distracting.

Requires care on the part of the presenter if use is to be effective.

Advantages

Immensely flexible.

Slides can be built up in stages to show underlying detail.

Can be written on during a presentation.

Images can be altered and adapted (but should be used with care as requires water based pens and can be very messy)

Does not require a darkened room.

Size of image can be altered.

Presenter faces audience at all times.

Slides much easier to prepare than for other systems (such as 35mm projectors).

35mm Slide projector

Disadvantages

Strict blackout essential.

Lack of personal contact between presenter and audience combined with dark room can have strong soporific effect.

No room for flexibility in the direction which the talk may take.
For best results an automatic control mechanism for the projector
   and for lighting levels is necessary.
Expensive.
Slide preparation can be troublesome and take up much time.

Advantages

Excellent for highly detailed drawings and photographs.

Gramophone/Tape players

Advantages

Indispensible for demonstrating a unique sound or performance.
Can be used to imitate phone calls etc. to add realism to an
   example/case study.

Disadvantages

Bad for putting over detailed information.
Very limited in scope. (You should not normally consider other than
   for the purposes listed under 'advantages'.)

Video

Undoubtedly, the best use of video is in the area of practical skills
teaching. The trainee is filmed attempting to carry out the desired task.
The video is then played back and the instructor points out where the
trainee has gone wrong. This direct visual feedback is far more
powerful than any type of verbal explanation (also, very good for
improving your golf). If you are considering attending a course on
presentation skills, don't even consider a course unless it uses video
playback techniques.

   However, most business presentations don't include practical training. The most likely use of video is as an alternative medium for
putting over a point. It is unlikely that you will consider actually
making a video to use as part of your presentation (although if you are
engaged in a major training programme it may be worth considering),
but there are a number of very good ready-made videos on the market,
covering a wide range of subjects. If you are able to find a video that is
relevant (and it must be) it is usually a good idea to use it.

Advantages

Audio-visual presentation is effective because it appeals to two
   senses at once.

The quality of presentation is first class.

Specialised techniques are available to the video producer that would be prohibitively expensive in the classroom.

Introduction of a completely different medium helps to break up the presentation and relieve boredom.

Disadvantages

No room for flexibility in direction or approach.

Topics covered by the video may be in a different order to that planned, and cause sequencing problems with the rest of the presentation.

Equipment is expensive.

Monitors must be positioned within a short distance of every position in the audience.

Synchronised Tape/slide show, Film

These methods don't have the instant playback facility of video, but otherwise the considerations are similar. One of the main drawbacks of the film or slide show is that a darkened room is required. In practice the market is now dominated by video, the quality of material usually being much better.

Computer assisted learning

Otherwise known as CBT (Computer Based Training), these methods are usually employed as an alternative to presentation techniques, the advantage being that training can take place as and when the trainee is available. Production of CBT material is prohibitively expensive as it requires the use of experienced programmers in order to produce the material. It will not be considered further here.

When should aids be used?

Aids are used for three main purposes:

To give emphasis
To help explain a point
To make something easier to remember

In your presentation there will be certain points which you regard as important. Use aids to stress these points. *Avoid using aids to explain less important points.* You must find some way of making the important points stand out. By reserving your use of aids for the important points you give a clear indication to the audience as to what is important, and what is not.

Use an aid to help explain something which is conceptually difficult. Your aid should show a picture, or diagram of some kind. Using aids to express analogies or make comparisons can be very effective. (cf. the water pump/electric current diagram in chapter 1.)

If you are anxious that the audience should remember something — use an aid to drive the point home. If you can use a picture of some kind, so much the better.

Which type of aid should be used?

To present a picture, a diagram or a straightforward statement of some kind, the Overhead Projector is usually the most effective medium.

Don't use a slide projector, unless you have to show photographs or diagrams of unusually intricate detail. Dark rooms can have sleep inducing powers which often prove irresistible and should be avoided whenever possible.

If you are making a statement of continuing relevance, put it up where it can be seen permanently. For instance, if you are going to cover three main questions, put them up on a white board or flipchart. You can then use the Overhead projector for the remainder of your visual aids, turning back to the questions on the flipchart as you reach the appropriate stages. This type of approach gives added emphasis to the structure of the presentation, so that the audience always 'know where they are' and feel comfortable.

If you intend to invite responses from the audience a white board or a flipchart is a good idea. You should put points from the audience up where they can be seen and leave them there. This encourages the audience to believe that you are concerned about their points. So choose an aid which you will not need for the rest of the presentation.

For points which have only passing relevance, choose an aid which can be dispensed with quickly so that the information will not be left hanging there (such as an Overhead Projector, which can be switched off, or a Flipchart, which can be flipped over). Irrelevant visual aids are an uncomfortable distraction for the audience.

Avoid using a lot of aids that require you to stand with your back to the audience (writing on a flipchart or white board). Showing the audience your back is an extremely negative psychological signal. If a circumstance should arise where a lot of writing is required (e.g. taking a lot of audience response), use a colleague to do the writing.(You can use somebody from the audience, but this might be looked on as unfair for the person that is picked. Using the audience in this way on a long course, where people are picked in turn is more acceptable, and can even improve the course by increasing the level of audience participation)

Try to be imaginative. If you think of an unusual way to emphasise a point with an aid, *use it!*

Designing a visual aid

Avoid using a lot of text. It is all right to emphasise key statements by using an aid which simply restates the key point. But if you find that most of your aids have just text on them, it is time to rethink your approach.

Never use an aid which is cluttered with text. It is acceptable to 'unfold' a list of up to about eight points by gradually exposing an OHP (overhead projector) slide line by line. But it would be unwise to present the same slide in its entirety on first sight.

All text should be in large letters which can easily be read from the back of the room. Test an aid before you use it.

Vary the way in which you present the information. If you can, use some slides to build-up a picture and some which are uncovered in stages. Try to use several types of aids during the presentation. You will usually be using the overhead projector for most of your aids, try to include some use of other aids to break the monotony.

Use colour. Colourful images are impressive and easily remembered. But don't overdo it! Tasteless garishness will put the audience off.

Be fussy about the quality of the graphics. If you are unable to draw good quality diagrams, get someone who can to do it for you.

Be consistent throughout the presentation and follow generally accepted conventions (red for danger etc.). A good way to achieve consistency is to use standard logos or characters in related situations. This helps the audience see the link (aiding the Gestaltic pattern-forming type of learning)

As an example we will design some aids to be used at the begining of the talk on the Purchase Order system, continuing the example that we used in the previous chapter.

Example Aids for the Purchase order talk

From the material covered in chapter four, you know that it is crucial to emphasise the message and the structure at the beginning of the talk. Because of this, we will use three aids to put over the message and the structure.

First, we state the message in simple, direct terms using an overhead slide (figure 5.2). Note the use of graphic elements (the box and arrow) in an attempt to increase the impact.

Next, we put up the structure (Figure 5.3), using a flip-chart this time so that we can refer back as we reach each stage of the presentation.

To consolidate the structure, we can use an overhead slide, showing the context of the talk (figure 5.4). This overhead emphasises the structure because it shows clearly the three different areas which will

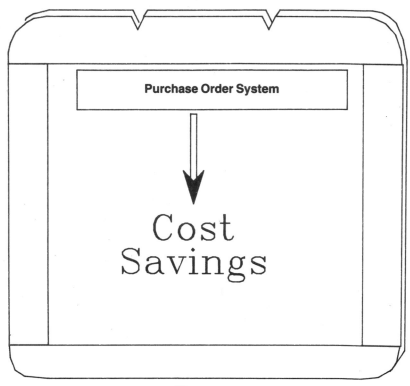

Figure 5.2

be covered. To make the structure stand out even more, the slide is in the form of an overlay, so that each system can be shown and talked about separately.

The overhead in figure 5.4, not only consolidates the structure, but also performs two other important functions. It highlights *relationships* between the areas to be covered, thus aiding the Gestaltic pattern-forming. It also helps set *ground rules* (so if you get a question on the consequences for the Widget production sub-system, you can say, 'At the beginning I showed quite clearly the three areas which I am prepared to cover to-day, If you see me at the end of the presentation I would be happy to look into it for you.')

The next job is to produce aids for each of the three sections of the talk and for the recap. By way of example we will just produce an aid for the first section and one for the recap.

If you look back at the structure for the talk, on page 38, you will see that the main objective for the first section concerns stock savings. From the minor objectives you can see that these savings are brought

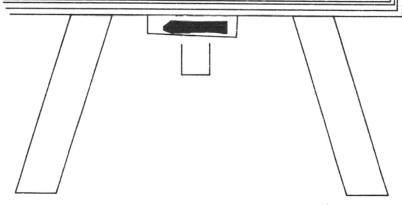

Figure 5.3

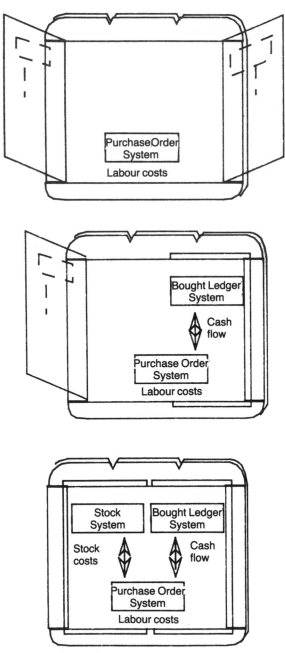

Figure 5.4

about through a stock-related trigger mechanism activated by a link between the stock and purchase order systems.

We can show this diagrammatically, by using a stock pile, with an arrow at a certain level pointing to a purchase order (see figure 5.5). A neat way of showing the relation between the two systems is to show a parallel diagram showing the overnight tape transfer (assuming for the moment that it is a tape transfer). The second part of the slide is uncovered when the first part has been explained.

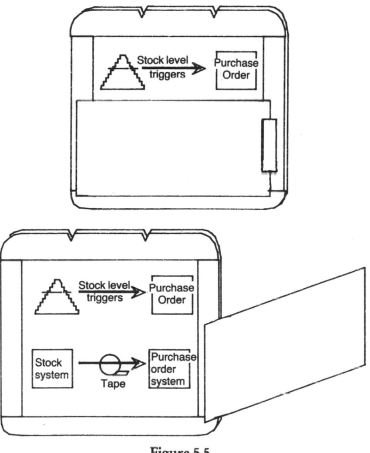

Figure 5.5

For the recap at the end of the talk, a slide similar to that shown in figure 5.6 could be used. The message is hammered home by ending the presentation with the key point — cost savings. The slide re-emphasises the structure by showing the costs in three parts.

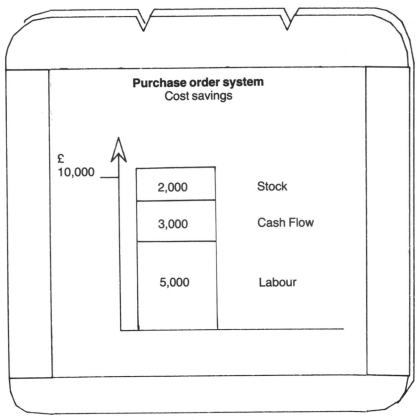

Figure 5.6

When you have designed your visual aids, the next stage is to make them up.

Making an Overhead Projector slide

To make overhead projector slides you will need:

1. Acetate sheets.
2. Special pens (the permanent type are much less messy).
3. Masking tape (not sellotape which becomes brittle with age).
4. Methylated spirits (to clean grease spots).
5. Cardboard mounts.
6. Templates for tracing or 'Letraset' letters.

In addition you may find useful:

1. Self-adhesive coloured film for blocks of colour.
2. A sharp knife

To make a slide proceed as follows:

1. Mark out the boundaries of the cardboard mount on a plain sheet of paper.
2. Sketch out the contents of the slide on the paper and tape the paper to the desk.
3. Tape an acetate sheet to the cardboard mount.
4. Position the mount over the sketch on the plain sheet, with the notches at the top. Tape the cardboard mount to the desk.

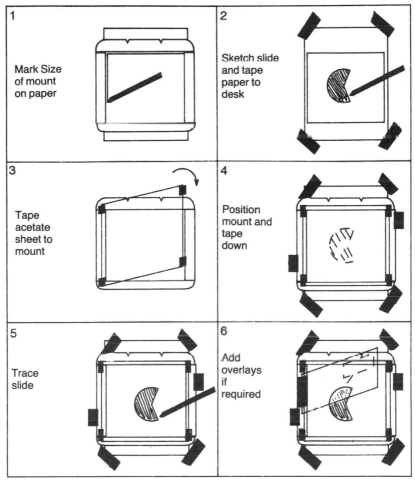

Figure 5.7

5. Trace out the contents of the slide.
6. For long lasting slides tape a second piece of acetate over the original picture.

These procedures are summarised in figure 5.7.

To make a build-up slide use additional pieces of acetate, using a short length of masking tape as a hinge (see figure 5.4). Similarly, you can attach pieces of plain card to uncover a slide in stages (figure 5.5).

Summary of chapter five – Use of aids

Why do we need to use aids?

Seventy five percent of knowledge learning is through the visual sense.

I hear and I forget. I see and I remember. I do and I understand.

When to use aids

To give emphasis.

To help explain a point.

To make something easy to remember.

Not for unimportant points.

Which aids to use?

Whiteboard/Flipchart for interactive sessions with the audience, putting up a structure, audience questions.

35mm slide projector for detailed diagrams, photographs.

Overhead Projector as standard aid for most purposes.

Tape/Gramophone for special sounds, case studies.

Designing an aid

Use pictures wherever possible.

Restrict the amount of text.

Easily legible from the back of the room.

Use colour.

Vary the type of aid used.

Be conscious of image quality.

Use logos, standard characters for consistency.

Use build-up and reveal techniques creatively.

CHAPTER 6

Preparing the Notes

What is the function of your Presentation notes?

To be a script of what you are going to say?

To a certain extent, yes. But there is a much more important function.

The presentation notes discipline your actions. If you were left to roam free, the likelihood is that you would talk at great length with little interruption or interaction with the audience. If you did this, the presentation would be very boring.

A good set of notes forces you to take every opportunity to involve the audience by prompting you to ask questions, invite responses and use aids.

In this chapter we will show you how to construct notes which ensure that you give a lively, interactive presentation. We will also show you how to present the detailed content of your talk in the most effective way. First, we look at the requirements of the presentation, then consider the layout of the notes and finally show you how to write the notes.

Requirements of the presentation

As we said above, good notes will force you to involve the audience. But how much audience participation should there be? It will depend to a certain extent on the purpose of the presentation. If the purpose of the presentation is to instruct, there should be a high level of audience involvement. For example, when teaching staff to use a new system, it is vital that staff can use the system properly, if you are to capitalise on the investment. The learning process must be closely controlled to have maximum effect. The audience must be involved at every opportunity and tested at each stage.

In this instructional type of presentation, the percentage of time which should be devoted to audience activities is surprisingly high. Studies have shown that the learning process is most effective when the time of the presenter is allocated, on average, as follows:

Activity	Percentage of time
Direct instruction	36
Questioning	46
Giving support	14
Demonstrating	4
	100%

From the figures above you can see that the amount of time spent in giving direct instruction should be just a little over a third of the total time available.

If the purpose of the presentation is to inform, then a lower level of involvement is permissible. For example, if you are briefing senior management, the audience will already be motivated, and will not take kindly to intensive questioning.

If the purpose of your talk is to present the findings of an impartial study you will leave the bulk of the questioning to the audience, as they will most certainly be keen to establish the validity of your conclusion. If you are trying to persuade the audience then you must encourage them to question you, but control the line of questioning to your advantage. (This approach will be tempered by the degree of faith that you have in your argument!)

How can the notes be used to stimulate interaction? By scripting the audience's activities as well as your own. The best way to do this is to use a layout which forces you to consider audience activities.

Choosing a layout

First, we will look at a suitable layout for an instructional presentation.

Training theorists say that there are two ways to regard a trainer and his trainees. The first is to look upon the trainer as a resource which provides the training requirements of the group. The second is to look upon the group as a resource and to regard the trainer as the manager of that resource. If you use the first approach you are wasting the majority of the available resource. Needless to say, the second approach is always given as the preferred option. When you are preparing the notes for an instructional presentation, this is a useful philosophy to keep in mind.

For an instructional presentation, the layout of the notes should give as much space to the audience's activities as it does to the presenter's activities. In addition, you should be able to see at a glance where aids are to be used. A good layout is as follows:

Presenter	Audience	Aids

The great advantage of this layout, is that it gives an instant picture of the extent of audience involvement. If large areas of open space appear in the middle column of your notes, you know that you have to bring in more audience-centred activities. Similarly, if there are long gaps in the Aids column, you should consider whether you could be using additional aids.

If you are giving an informative presentation, the amount of audience participation will not be so great. The format used above could be modified to reflect this.

Presenter	Audience	Aids

The same layout could be used for a persuasive presentation. If you are giving a presentation following the scientific form you may be able to dispense with an audience column altogether, but this decision should be approached with care. Presentation of data can be inherently uninteresting and you may find it necessary to manufacture some kind of audience involvement to maintain interest.

We have been discussing the benefits of using columns for the main body of the talk, but what about the heading?

It is important to keep a record of the purpose of the talk and any assumptions you have made in its preparation. If you wish to use the talk at a later stage, a short summary of these details will make your task immensely easier.

What sort of details do you need to record? The most obvious is the title of the presentation, so at the top of the page should be the General Objective. The next information of interest will be some kind of record about what the talk is supposed to achieve. So there should be a list of Specific Objectives. You will also need to know what kind of audience the talk is suitable for. So a list of Prerequisites must be present.

For practical purposes, you will need to know how much time the talk takes up and what aids are required. A note of the duration of the talk and the equipment requirements should be somewhere in the heading. A pro-forma heading would look something like the example in figure 6.1.

It is a good idea to make copies of a pro-forma title sheet, together with a stack of copies of continuation sheets. *The key to successful preparation is self discipline.* If you have paper available which has the

General Objective _____

_____

Specific Objectives: At the end of this presentation, the listener will
be able to:

_____
_____
_____
_____
_____

Prerequisites: _____

_____

Duration: _____ Aids: _____

Presenter	Audience	Aids

Figure 6.1

correct layout, there is less temptation to be sloppy and write
inadequate presentation notes.

Writing the notes

How much detail should go into your notes? Some people get very
steamed up over this, not knowing whether to write notes verbatim or
to use only the broadest of headings.

As you gain experience in giving presentations you will discover the

How much detail should go into your notes?

Figure 6.2

right type of notes for you. But to start with there are certain considerations which you should bear in mind.

When you give a presentation you are a person talking to other people. You should act and behave naturally. It is impossible to be yourself if you are reading a set of notes word for word.

You are talking to people about a subject which you know and understand. They have come to benefit from your wisdom. If you were asked to explain something to a colleague, you would not write out your explanation meticulously first. You wouldn't need to. It is the same when you give a presentation. You should plan the substance of what you are going to say, but let the form of words that you use come naturally.

The notes form your detailed plan.

When you are giving the presentation, you will not want to have to spend a large amount of time wading through your notes. They should be clear and brief. If you have a detailed set of facts which you wish to impart, or if you are going to use a detailed example, don't include the detail in your notes. For detailed information use a supplementary sheet which can be copied and distributed to the audience.

When you are writing the notes, remember that the audience has a limited attention span. If you keep introducing new material at a fast pace, the your listeners' short term memory will suffer from overload and the audience will switch off. Keep your major points well spaced from each other. Use the intervening periods to talk around a point, coming at it from different directions and using examples.

In a great piece of music the tremendous climaxes owe much of their effect to the contrast with the quiet, inobtrusive passages. And similarly, the impressive moments of your presentation will be set off by a measured pre-amble.

Remember that when you are giving the talk, your only reference to the notes will be an occasional glance down. In these circumstances, even the briefest of sentences can be difficult to read quickly. You can help yourself by highlighting the essential phrases in sentences (by writing in a different colour, or using underlining).

Look for key points in the notes and give them special emphasis. This will help you to give emphasis in your delivery.

To illustrate the principles which we have been discussing, we will continue with our example talk on the Purchase Order System.

The notes in figures 6.3 cover the beginning of the talk and the section on stock control.

As the purpose of the talk is to inform, and not to instruct, the column for audience activity is fairly narrow (but nevertheless important).

At the beginning of the notes, no special markings have been used. This is for a good reason: at the beginning of your talk you will not be looking at the notes! But you must write down what you are going to do at the beginning of a talk, to clear it in your own mind and for future re-use. On the second and third pages essential phrases have been underlined. The important points are surrounded by boxes.

Note the way in which the important information has been spread. At the beginning of the talk the Message is given. There is then some time spent in building up to the next important point, the introduction of the new stock feature, using Overhead slide 3. This order is used deliberately to ensure a reasonable space of time between important points.

Look at the way in which opportunities are taken to involve the audience. If a standard sheet of paper had been used to produce the notes it is unlikely that the questions to the audience would have been built in. But the looming white space of an extra column provides the incentive to look for interaction.

The talk could easily have been given using just one type of aid, a flipchart, or an overhead projector. But three types of aid have purposely been included to introduce variety. Note also the instruction to rub out irrelevant information on the third page. And the use of the flipchart to emphasize the structure of the talk.

Now you are ready to consider the final stage, giving the talk. But first read through the summary at the end of this chapter.

General Objective   _To give an appreciation of the cost benefits_
                     of the purchase order system

Specific Objectives: At the end of this presentation, the listener will
                     be able to:
         List the areas in which cost cuttings will be achieved
         State the amount of saving that will be achieved in each area
         Explain how the system will lead to lower stock levels
         Explain how the system will improve cash flow
         Compare the labour requirements & costs for the old & new systems

Prerequisites: _The audience must: have basic accounting knowledge_
                and be familiar with existing systems and basic DP concepts

Duration: _45 mins_ Aids: _O'head projector, F/chart & whiteboard_

Presenter	Audience	Aids
Let audience get drink etc., Make introductions, give brief timetable, point out toilets etc.	Get drink etc	
While audience settle, state the general objective. Give the message. The purchase order system will reduce costs.		OH 1
Uncover, prepared F/chart showing structure.		F/ch
Explain context of talk using OHP.		OH 2
Invite initial questions from audience. Ask for specific problems caused by the purchase order system, so that any individual grievances or concerns can be covered. Mark up on board.	Respond with grievances, concerns.	White board
Outline the advantages of controlled stock levels		

Figure 6.3

Presenter	Audience	Aids
Talk through recent <u>difficulties in getting</u> <u>warehouse space</u>. Ask the Warehouse manager to give example confirming problems.	Response from Mr. Stoneit.	
Outline <u>present procedures</u> for re-ordering stock		
Point out <u>difficulties in present system</u>:		
Relies on <u>clerical procedures</u> being up to date (mention historical trouble with backlogs)		
Needs <u>constant monitoring</u> to work properly.		
Ask audience if troubles had been experienced from clerical delays.	Respond with troubles.	
<u>Speculate</u> on ideal solution. Ask audience to give <u>requirements</u> of an ordering system that meets their needs. Put up on F/chart (behind structure).	Respond with requirements.	F/ch
<u>Introduce the new stock feature</u> using OHP slide		OH 3
<u>Compare requirements</u> of audience with features offered by new system.		
Perform <u>rough calculation</u> on blank half of white board, substantiating figure of £2,000 in savings.		White board
Go through any relevant <u>audience points</u> up on white board.		White board
Ask for <u>final questions</u> on Stock system link and deal with them.	Respond.	

Figure 6.3

Presenter	Audience	Aids
Recap on important points. Put up slide again and emphasize figure of £2,000 in savings.		OH 3
Rub out calculations on white board, and audience points that have been dealt with		
Turn Flipchart to page with structure on. Point out that the first topic has been dealt with and read out second topic; Cash flow savings.		F/ch

Figure 6.3

Summary of chapter 6 – Preparing the notes

Function of the presentation notes

To provide an outline script.

To force you to involve the audience and make good use of aids.

Requirements of the presentation

For an instructional presentation, plan for a high degree of audience involvement.

For an informative presentation, plan to involve the audience, but avoid detailed questioning, which could be regarded as hostile (or cheeky).

Choosing a layout
Use a separate column for audience activities and for aids.

Writing the notes

Write brief notes.

Underline essential phrases and highlight key points.

Keep your important points apart from each other.

CHAPTER 7

Giving the Presentation

It takes much longer to prepare a presentation than it does to give one, and the coverage given to preparation in this book reflects this. But good preparation is not, in itself, enough. Just as a well presented talk which is badly prepared will surely fail, so will an immaculately prepared presentation which is badly delivered.

In this chapter we will take you through all the stages in executing a presentation.

Before the presentation starts

Check everything. Is the room big enough? Are there electrical points in the right places? Has the room been booked for the right day and time? Is all the necessary equipment available? Are there spare bulbs for the overhead projector? Can you set up the room the way you want to? Have the audience been notified? Is there going to be a disco next door? Can you get there in time? Will the set-up of the room be changed before you are going to use it?

One factor worth stressing is Environment. The temperature of the room should be neither cold nor stifling, and the atmosphere clean and fresh. The seats occupied by the audience should be comfortable. You may feel that these factors are outside your responsibility. But they can have a dramatic effect on the way people receive your presentation. However good a performance you put on, if your listeners leave the room with aching backs, running noses, cold feet and stiff necks; they aren't going to feel that they enjoyed themselves. And you are the person responsible for their suffering. So it is wise to do everything you can to make sure that the environment is comfortable. (These days smoking is often regarded as intensely annoying by some people. It may be worth your while to find out the smoking habits of your audience, and, if necessary, make arrangements for smokers to sit in a separate, well-ventilated area.)

Needless to say you can never be sure of everything one hundred per cent. And nearly every experienced presenter will be able to quote an experience where the most fastidious preparation was frustrated by the completely unforeseeable. (It's amazing how often a million-to-one chance can occur.) But there is one thing you can be certain of. If you don't check, something will go wrong. And you'll look a right idiot when it does.

Non-Verbal Behaviour

What do we mean by non-verbal behaviour? Put simply, what you *do* rather than what you say. Or to use the common modern phrase: your body language.

But is it *that* important? If the talk is interesting won't a kindly audience overlook it if you keep doing the wrong things? — *No.*

There are certain instincts ingrained in every human being. For the most part they go suppressed and unnoticed. But they affect the way we react to everything.

Deep, genetic processes in the brain have been passed down through the generations since man evolved from the ape (or yeti, or whatever). These processes constantly monitor the signals received by the senses, looking for signs of hostility or friendship. Certain body actions by you will trigger adverse emotional reponses by your audience. Of course, the audience will not see your gestures as threatening, they will just be aware that they don't like you, and that they are not enjoying themselves.

Illustrations of the type of signals you may unconsciously give to the audience are given in figures 7.1 and 7.2.

In general, you should try to send positive body language signals. Positive signals are:

Leaning towards
Physical proximity
Smiling
Eye contact
Open arms/hands/palms

Of course, some of these signals aren't always useful in the context of a presentation. Conducting a presentation 'leaning towards' an audience isn't really possible unless you bolt your feet to the floor beforehand, and even if you went to this length it is very dubious whether you would gain an advantage!

It isn't necessary to have a deep understanding of body language to be a successful presenter. But there are certain rules you should follow.

Don't flirt with your audience and, if you are female, avoid wearing overtly alluring clothes. Sexual instincts are very powerful and will completely swamp any other motivation you may have nurtured in the

The two figures above are identical except for the position of the hands.
Both show open palms, but the figure on the right looks a lot less threatening than the figure on the left. Why?
To find the answer we must look at the way early man attacked his enemies.

Early man was a hunting carnivore. In order to compete with animals of much greater physical abilities, he used his superior intelligence and fought with weapons. The classical method of attack was to hold the weapon above the head and bring it down with force on the victim. Our legacy from this is that, even today, our ancestral memories perceive similar actions as being hostile.

Figure 7.1

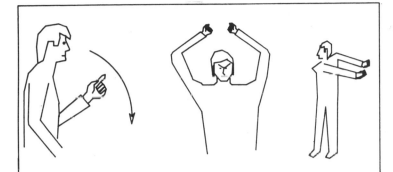

The postures shown above all have a hostile or a negative impact
and are derived, to a greater or lesser extent, from the attacking
posture of early man.
The dominant finger-wagging comes from the downward sweep
of the overhead blow. The hands-over-head display of anger is
derived from the pre-strike position. The posture for rejection has
some of its impact because the hands are raised, palm
downwards, only a tentative link with the full-blooded swipe, but
nevertheless effective.

In the same way that a downward sweeping palm shows a hostile
signal, an upturned palm shows the absence of aggression. The
first posture above shows helplessness, the second posture is
used to welcome guests.
Note that not only are the hands shown to be non-aggressive, but
the body is shown open and defenceless.

Figure 7.1

As well as using weapons for attacking purposes, early man learnt how to use shields to defend himself.
If a rival tribe approached with shields raised, it signalled that they were expecting conflict, i.e. that they had hostile intentions.
Early man therefore came to identify a shielded person as an enemy.

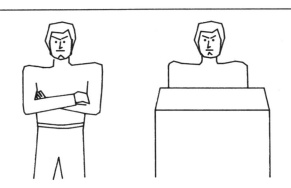

Our instincts still tell us that a shield is used to protect an aggressor.
The shield can be conveyed by posture, such as the folded arms of the figure on the left, or the shield can be a physical barrier as shown by the figure on the right.
Whilst neither of these positions have the strong, aggressive effect of those shown in Figure 7.1, they will nevertheless stimulate negative feelings in an audience.

Figure 7.2

Many animals, including early man, attempt to avoid conflict by frightening off a potential aggressor. To do this they have to look more dangerous than they really are.
One of the ways in which man could look dangerous was by inflating his chest and spreading his arms to present a much wider profile.

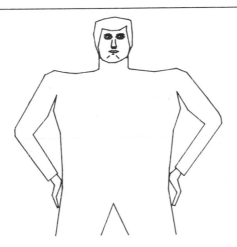

Modern man uses exactly the same technique as early man when he wishes to convince others of his dominance.
The characteristic posture is achieved by breathing in to expand the chest and by placing the hands squarely on the hips to maximise the size of the body presented to his potential opponent.

Figure 7.2

audience. Whatever views you hold about sexism, the reaction to an attractive member of the opposite sex is a fact that you have to live with. (There are occasions when, if done subtly, the sexual instinct can be used to your advantage. For example, a story was told about a lecturer with a class that were habitually late returning from lunch. One day, just before lunch, he accidentally put up the first slide of the afternoon's session. The slide was entitled, 'The art of seduction'. When the class returned, early and keen to get on with the afternoon's work, just as they expected, the topic to be discussed had been changed to something a little more relevant to their course. But none of them had taken the chance of arriving late for the session!)

Look at your audience. If you are speaking to a small group switch your gaze from one pair of eyes to another, giving equal attention to all. If you have a full room, don't concentrate on the people at the front; give equal attention to the people in the middle and at the back. With a very large audience, you will find that you cannot 'lock in' to people individually; in this case sweep your eyes around the room from one group in the audience to another.

Don't be afraid to smile. When there is opportunity for humour, take it. Of course, you shouldn't overdo it. If you keep cracking jokes the audience will not be able to concentrate on what you have to say. Similarly, an occasional natural smile is more effective than a perpetual toothpaste-commercial grin.

Don't talk to the wall. When you are writing something on a white board or flipchart, the room seems extremely silent and there is a strong temptation to just keep on talking. *Don't*. Take time to make sure that you write clearly and then turn around to make your point. You can help yourself by avoiding activities that require you to spend long periods writing when you write your Presentation notes. If there is a lot of writing to be done — get somebody else to do it (see also page 46).

Keep your hands down and don't wag your finger. The natural way for one human to attack another is to raise the arm in the air. A gesture of this kind is psychologically unsettling.

Don't put things between you and the audience. Keep your notes on a desk (or table) to one side (see Figure 7.3).

Avoid distracting mannerisms. If it itches don't scratch it — suffer. If you have access to a video, get someone to make a recording of a trial presentation. You will be surprised at the habits which you have that you are unaware of.

Keep your movements simple. Don't dash around from one end of

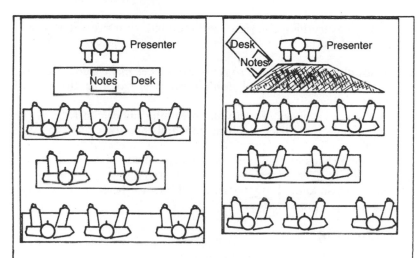

Never allow barriers to come between you and the audience. In the diagram on the left, the presenter stands behind a large desk. Subconsciously, the audience sees this as a hostile signal, and it will be difficult for the presenter to develop a rapport.
The correct approach is shown on the right hand side, where the shaded area is kept clear.

Figure 7.3

the room to another. If you feel that you should move, a relaxed change of position will add to the natural atmosphere of the presentation.

After giving you the previous set of rules the next statement may seem something of a contradiction, but it is the most important rule of all. **Be yourself**. At the most basic level you should remember that you are just a person talking to other people. If you try and pretend otherwise you will come unstuck. So remember the rules and practise until they come naturally. But don't be so concerned about getting the rules right that you become a robot. Being natural is the most important rule of all.

Before we move on, there is one thing we should mention as an aside. Whereas you can use body language to positive effect yourself, don't rely on the body language of others to make judgements. Postures *may* be a good indication, but studies have shown that, often, the stance taken is more related to tension than to any particular mood.

Voice projection and diction

This could have been included as part of the previous section, but it is sufficiently important to merit separate mention.

If you get everything else right, and mumble, your presentation will be a dismal failure.

Speak loudly and clearly. Project your voice, make sure that you sound the end of words and don't drop your voice at the end of sentences.

Don't say 'um' or 'er'. Keep your breathing under control.

Ask if people at the back can hear you, and encourage them to say if they can't.

Look to the back of the room regularly; people look different if they are straining to hear. Make sure that they aren't.

Now that you know how to stand, and how to speak, you are ready to start giving a presentation.

The Opening

You may have been lectured as a child about the importance of first impressions and a smart appearance. It is certainly true about giving a presentation. The impression you make in the first few minutes will stick with the audience throughout the whole presentation.

How do you start? First you must get the body language right. Move away from your desk and towards the audience. Smile, open your arms in a 'welcome' gesture (Figure 7.1) and then put your hands at your sides. As you start to speak look at everybody in the room. If it is a small group, slowly turn your head around making contact with each pair of eyes in turn.

You can spend some time, in this forward position. You are making friends with the audience. Make sure that you know the beginning of the talk thoroughly, so that you don't have to retreat quickly back to your notes.

What is the first thing that you talk about? Address the audience's concerns. What do we mean by concerns? A useful way of looking at it is to use Maslow's pyramid of human needs.

Abraham Maslow represented human needs by grouping them in a pyramid, as shown in figure 7.4. The reason for using this structure is that needs on a higher level are unlikely to be considered as being important unless the needs on a lower level have been satisfied.

To take an obvious example, if someone is desperately hungry, they are not going to take much notice of your talk on ancient Egyptian customs, however gripping your delivery.

For you to receive the full attention of your audience, you must eradicate any basic concerns that they may have. By 'basic' concerns, we mean those that come on the lower levels of Maslow's pyramid.

Make sure that there are no worries that will distract their attention from what you have to say. Let them know where the toilets are,

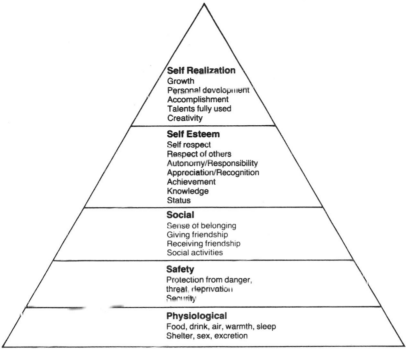

Figure 7.4*

where the coffee machine is, what time tea breaks and lunch breaks are. These sort of activities may seem trivial, but it can be guaranteed that if no mention of a break has been made and stomachs start rumbling, the majority of the audience will be waiting for food, not listening to what you say.

When you begin to talk to the audience you will get a strange feeling about your arms. Instead of feeling natural and relaxed at your side, they will feel unnaturally unoccupied. You can overcome this by planning to do something useful with your arms, without letting your gesticulations get out of control. For instance when you state where the coffee machine is, it is acceptable to point to it. When you run off the times of the tea and coffee breaks, count them off unobtrusively on your fingers, tapping the fingers of the left hand with the index finger of the right, holding your hands down low.

Next, set the ground rules for the presentation. Explain fully your intentions and the scope of the presentation. This is especially important if you are talking to senior management.

For example, if you intend to poll reaction to some tentative

* Figure 7.4 is adapted from 'Hierarchy of Needs' in a 'Theory of Motivation' in *Motivation and Personality*, A. H. Maslow (2nd ed., 1970, Harper and Row)

proposals and provoke further thought on a subject, say so clearly. If management disagree, you can welcome their comments and say that the main purpose of the presentation has been accomplished. If you gave the same presentation without making that point first, it could be a disaster. Unless you state otherwise, the audience will regard everything you say as your opinion of the facts. If they disagree with you, they will shoot you down in flames. And saying *after* the event that you just intended to get their opinion will not ring true. You will be discredited. So, if you are on shaky ground at all: cover yourself well before you start talking.

There is one thing you should bear in mind when setting ground rules. It is your presentation and you can set whatever rules you want. If you make a statement at this stage, nobody will argue, whatever their position in the firm. You control the room and you have an immense psychological advantage over the audience. If you set a rule at the beginning you can enforce it easily with a brief comment, 'As I said before we started, we are not going into that area . . . '. If you try to set rules half way through a presentation, you will lose credibility with the audience and you will lose control of the presentation. So anticipate problems with a difficult audience and take care of them at the outset, when you have the power.

At this stage the audience is settled and waiting to hear what you have got to say. You will never again have them so consciously attentive and receptive. So give them the message and ram it home good. You have something interesting to tell them and they are going to *want* to know about it. Sell it to them now and you have them motivated for the rest of the presentation. Use a visual aid. A big, slick multi-coloured one if you can.

Give them the message
Show them the visual
Pause, and let it sink in

Now, you have got them well and truly with you. Give them the structure. Ideally it will be in three parts, which, again, you can count off on your fingers to occupy your arms. Show them the structure in writing and emphasise it. Techniques used to make a point are covered in the next section.

Making a point

In the chapter on preparing the notes, we said that the presentation should be structured around high points, separated by low-key material of a supportive nature. How do you signal to the audience that you have come to one of the high points? How do you make a point?

Slow down your delivery.
Put the key word(s) at the end of the sentence.
Pause before and after the key word(s).
Repeat.

For example, the sentence:

The Giant Axon of the squid is the largest nerve fibre found in the animal world.

has the important words at the front. It would be much better remembered if put like this:

The largest nerve fibre in the animal world is, <pause> the Giant Axon of the squid.

The effectiveness of this sentence increases markedly if repeated, using the same pause. Why? Because the second time the audience knows what you are going to say. When you pause members of the audience complete the sentence in their minds.
You say:

The largest nerve fibre in the animal world is, <pause>

The audience thinks:

The Giant Axon of the squid.

You say:

the Giant Axon of the squid.

Earlier in the book we said that it was important to create expectations and then confirm them. This use of pausing and repeating is a very good example of that technique.
You can also think of this type of phrasing in terms of behaviourist theory. If you consider the sentence as a Stimulus–Response unit, *The largest nerve fibre in the animal world is* becomes the stimulus and *The Giant Axon of the squid* is the response. By encouraging the audience to repeat the response mentally, you drive the point home. Skinner described this technique by saying: **The response is the agent of reinforcement.**
You should follow this example whenever you can. Use the response as the agent of reinforcement.

Set up a Stimulus–Response link
Give the stimulus
Let the audience respond
Confirm the response

When you use this technique the response of the audience doesn't have to be spoken. It is often more effective if, as in the example above, the audience makes the response mentally. This is especially the case if you are talking to senior executives who do not take kindly to being asked to chant in sing-song fashion!

The pause technique is also useful when asking questions.

Asking Questions

For a presentation to have life, the audience must be involved. And the easiest way to involve the audience is by asking questions. If you are talking to senior people the approach will be different to that used for an instructional presentation to junior staff.

When you ask a senior person a question, you are asking for the benefit of his invaluable opinion. Once you have made a few enquiries of the audience the ice is broken and subsequent comments will flow, without encouragement, thick and fast. It is down to you to control these questions. If you expect trouble from a highly voluble audience, you might consider placing restrictions on the questions in the ground rules that you set at the beginning. In addressing a senior group, you will inevitably lose some of the advantages of audience interaction, because of the necessity to keep things formal. Recognise this and compensate for it in other ways. Be enthusiastic in your delivery, concentrate your effort on the major points, make sure that your aids are of the highest quality and emphasise the structure of the talk.

When you are talking to junior staff, and the prime purpose of your talk is to instruct, your questions must be direct and searching. Keep your audience on its toes by asking questions frequently and at random. Don't look at the recipient until you have asked the question, ensuring that everyone in the audience listens attentively. When you have asked a question, pause and wait for the answer. If no answer is forthcoming give a clue and pause again. If no answer comes, give a heavier clue. If the answer is incorrect, try to steer the recipient towards the right answer. If no amount of prompting elicits the right reply, try to find something mitigating in the recipient's favour before passing the question on. It is in your interests to keep your audience motivated. When you recieve the correct reply, give praise and repeat the answer *using the exact words that the recipient of the question used*. Using the trainee's own words in this way can be highly motivating for the trainee. It is another application of the maxim: The response is the agent of reinforcement.

But what about when the boot is on the other foot, when the awkward questions are directed at you?

Handling Questions from the audience

You should be able to handle most of the questions you receive. If not, you are talking about the wrong subject. Sometimes though, in practice, it is impossible to avoid skating on thin ice, and if you find that you are you must make the best of it.

If you know the answer to a question, give it as clearly and simply as you can. When you have finished, ask the questioner if he is satisfied with the answer and take reasonable care to elaborate if necessary. If the questioner probes deeper and deeper, wasting too much time and distracting from the main body of the talk, offer to discuss the subject with him at the end.

If you do not know the answer to a question, never make it up. Make suitable apologies for not being able to answer straight away. Sometimes a little white lie doesn't hurt. 'I'm almost sure that I understand what you want to know, but there is a slight danger of confusion here and I would like to check on something first to guard against misleading you.' Always promise to give the answer eventually. If you can, find out during a break. When you are unable to answer questions immediately, make a list of the questions somewhere prominent, to reassure the audience that you care about what they want to know.

If questioning becomes too intense, stop taking questions until the end of the talk. It helps considerably if you have given yourself this option when you set the groundrules, so bear it in mind with potentially hostile audiences.

The degree of questioning you receive is a good indication of the mood of the audience, which is the subject of the next section.

Assessing the audience

Keep monitoring the behaviour of the audience to make sure that they are still 'with you'. If you are giving an instructional presentation, and you see someone's attention begin to drift, steer a few questions in that direction. If you are giving an informative presentation, focus in on the people drifting by locking your eyes on them, as if you are speaking to them personally. Ask their opinions on various points. Look for signs of uninterest, slumping in the chair, folded arms, yawning, failure to take notes, or at worst, whispered conversations. When you see evidence of this behaviour act as quickly as possible to involve the culprit in the presentation. Taking constructive steps to involve somebody is usually far more effective than rebuking them.

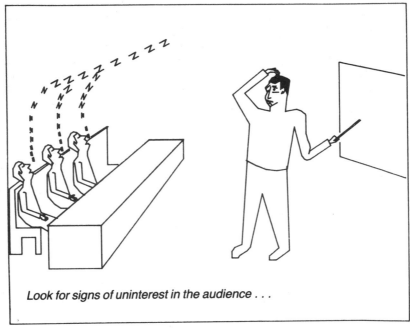

Look for signs of uninterest in the audience . . .

Figure 7.5

Using visual aids

When do you show an aid? Before you start to make the point or after? Either can be effective in its place. As a standard rule you will not go wrong if you introduce a point and then reinforce it by using an aid.

Remember that the audience cannot do two things at once. If you are talking to them, they can't concentrate on an aid. And if they are looking at an aid, they can't listen to you talking.

Introduce the subject. Make your point verbally, using pause and repeat techniques to help it sink in. The response is the agent of reinforcement. When you have made your point verbally, show the aid. *Keep quiet for a few seconds while the audience looks at the aid.* When the audience has assimilated the picture, guide them through it, using brief explanations as necessary. When you are satisfied that the point has been made *remove the aid.* An aid that has done its job, which is left visible, is a distraction to the audience.

When you use an aid make sure that it is visible to all the audience. The most commonly used aid is the overhead projector. Positioning the projector can be difficult, and, sometimes, you will inevitably have to compromise. Some useful techniques for positioning are shown in figure 7.6.

As the overhead projector is used so commonly, it is worth spending a little time discussing how it should be used.

One of the great advantages of the overhead projector is that it allows you to look at the audience as you use the device. Don't waste this advantage by turning to look at the screen as you put slides up. Use the stubs on the machine and the pre-locating holes on the slide frames to position your slides correctly. When you have to look at the slide look at the original on the machine in front of you. Spend most of your time looking at the audience.

If you need to point to anything on the slide, place a pencil on the slide itself. It will show as an impressive black arrow on the screen.

Don't use the slides as prompts. It is easy to fall into the habit of letting the slides control your presentation. Put up the slide; read it; ah! that's what comes next; talk through the slide; next slide up. They are visual aids not visual crutches. Follow your notes and use the aid in its place. Don't read out the slides (good aids should contain very little text anyway). What you say should complement the aid, not repeat it mindlessly.

When you have finished with a slide, switch the projector off Simply removing the slide isn't good enough. The big white square caused by a projector left switched on is a significant distraction to the audience. Always use this sequence:

Position your slide
Switch on
Show slide
Switch off
Remove slide

Skillful use of the overhead projector makes a huge difference to the professionalism of your performance.

The Freeze

There will come a time when you are about to say something when you suddenly get a mental block. You freeze up completely. The advice may seem a little obvious, but nevertheless true. *Don't panic!*

Look at your notes, find your place (which is usually about three pages away when this condition strikes) read what you have to say slowly, compose yourself and carry on. While you are doing this it seems as if an eternity of silence is passing. But don't let it get to you, the audience will not even notice it. What seems like hours to you is in reality often a few seconds. Don't try and bluff and bluster your way out of it. Always compose yourself and look at the notes. When it happens it seems like disaster, but take heart, it isn't. Other than that there is no more advice to give.

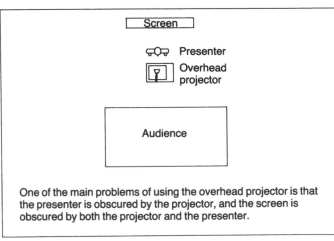

One of the main problems of using the overhead projector is that the presenter is obscured by the projector, and the screen is obscured by both the projector and the presenter.

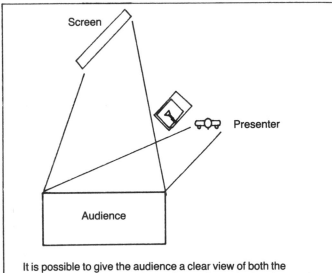

It is possible to give the audience a clear view of both the presenter and the screen by setting up the projector at an angle. Under this arrangement the presenter must move from behind the projector after positioning each slide. This method is still far from satisfactory as the distance between the presenter and the audience is increased, and some of the audience will see the screen at a very acute angle.

Figure 7.6

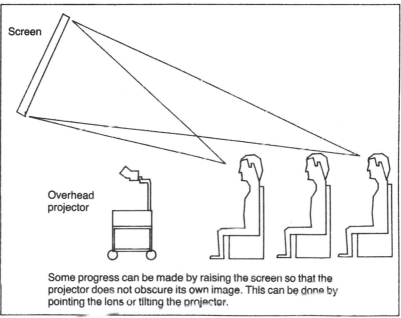

Screen

Overhead
projector

Some progress can be made by raising the screen so that the
projector does not obscure its own image. This can be done by
pointing the lens or tilting the projector.

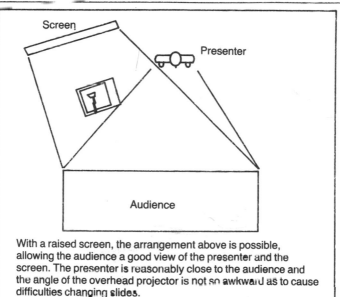

Screen

Presenter

Audience

With a raised screen, the arrangement above is possible,
allowing the audience a good view of the presenter and the
screen. The presenter is reasonably close to the audience and
the angle of the overhead projector is not so awkward as to cause
difficulties changing slides.

Shyness, nerves, lack of confidence

The best way of conquering nerves is to follow the advice given in the rest of this book. No, it doesn't mention anything about nerves specifically. But it does give you an awful lot of advice on technique. Far more than you could remember at once. But you should try. And when you do try you will find that you are so busy concentrating on your technique and your subject matter, that you don't have any time left to worry about nerves. The worst moments are those just before you start talking. So, if you find yourself turning to jelly (and most people do, nerves keep us on our toes) remind yourself that things will be all right when you start. As soon as you get up and start thinking that you should be close to the audience, that you should be sweeping your eyes around them, that you should be controlling your hands, that you should be avoiding distractions, that you should be doing all sorts of other things as well, suprisingly, you forget about nerves very quickly!

Remember, you are presenting the material, not yourself. Always look at the presentation as an objective exercise in communication.

And so, we come to ...

Finishing off the presentation

Remember that the last thing that the audience sees is the freshest thing that they take away with them. Next to the start, the finish is the most crucial part of the presentation.

Recap thoroughly. Spell out every important point that has been covered and in the order that you covered them. You've taken time to structure the talk properly, so use that structure as the basis for your recap. Prepare a special visual aid summarising your presentation.

It's easy for your enthusiasm to wane at the end of a long presentation. Don't let it!

Ask for final questions before you finish. Try and hold back an important point which you think will be the subject of a question. Use this to add impact to your finale. If someone is making a statement, not a question say, 'That's an interesting contribution,' and pass on quickly to someone else. If time is running out, always leave the brightest face for the final question, and go out with a flourish.

A final word

At the beginning we said that giving a presentation is like driving a car. Competence comes with a little time and patience. So don't be disappointed if you are not at Le Mans standard the first time you take the wheel!

Follow the advice given in this book, and, each time you give a presentation, look back at the things you got right and the things you got wrong. By learning from your mistakes, within a short space of time you will find you get most things right and you will grow in confidence and ability. Happy motoring!

Summary of chapter 7 – Giving the presentation

Preparation

Check everything!

Non-verbal behaviour

Don't flirt
Don't talk to the wall
Look at the audience
Keep your arms down and don't wag your finger
Don't put barriers between you and the audience
Avoid distracting mannerisms
Keep your movements simple
Above all — be yourself

The Opening

Go close to audience and make eye contact
Address audience's concerns (toilets, coffee,breaks etc.)
Set your ground rules
Give the message
Show the structure

Making a point

Slow delivery, key words last, pause at key words, repeat
The response is the agent of reinforcement
Create S–R link: Give stimulus: Elicit response: Confirm response

Asking questions

From senior staff: Ask opinions
From junior staff: direct searching questions
Pause and prompt to encourage response
Do not pre-locate visually
Give praise when due
Repeat answer in the trainee's own words

Handling questions

Answer clearly and ensure questioner is satisfied
If answer not known, promise to find out
Record unanswered questions in prominent place

Assessing the audience

Note signs of boredom (slumping, folding arms, yawning)

Involve people when attention drifts
Constructive involvement works better than a rebuke

Using visual aids

To reinforce a point you have made
Keep quiet when audience studies aid
Remove aid when you wish to resume talking
Ensure visible to whole audience
With OHP look at audience. Glance at projector. Don't look at screen
Use pencil as pointer on OHP
Always turn off OHP between slides
Position slide on OHP before turning on
Don't use aids as crutches, follow your notes

The freeze

Don't panic!
Don't bluff and bluster
Compose yourself and read your notes

Nerves

Concentrate on technique and subject matter

Finishing off

Recap thoroughly
Ask for questions
Hold a good point in reserve
Pick a bright face for last question to end well

APPENDIX

Suppliers of Visual Aids

Shops

a. boville wright
127–128, High Street, Uxbridge, Middx. UB8 1DJ. Tel: (0895) 38331/2
49, Queen Street, Maidenhead, Berks. SL6 7RX. Tel: (0628) 74656/7
16–18, Station Road, Gerrards Cross, Bucks. SL9 8EL. Tel: (0753) 884966

Suppliers:

Edding (Planmaster),
North Orbital Trading Estate,
Napsbury Lane,
St. Albans,
Herts. AL1 1XQ.

Film Sales Ltd.
145, Nathan Way,
Woolwich Industrial Estate,
London SE28 0BE.

International Tutor Machines,
15, Holder Road,
Aldershot,
Hants. GU12 4PU.

Letraset (UK) Ltd.,
195–203, Waterloo Road,
London SE1 8XJ.

Nobo Visual Aids Ltd.,
Alder Close,
Compton Industrial Estate,
Eastbourne,
Sussex BN23 6QB.

Staedtler UK,
Pontyclun,
Mid Glamorgan CF7 8YJ.

3M UK Plc,
3M House,
PO Box 1,
Bracknell,
Berks. RG12 1JU.

Index